PENGUIN BOOKS

AN ANZAC'S STORY

AN ANZAC'S STORY

ROY KYLE A.I.F.

Introduced and edited by
BRYCE COURTENAY

Books Alive is a Federal Government initiative
developed through the Australia Council

Penguin Books

Published by the Penguin Group
Penguin Books Australia Ltd
250 Camberwell Road, Camberwell, Victoria 3124, Australia
Penguin Books (NZ) Ltd
Cnr Rosedale and Airborne Roads, Albany, Auckland, New Zealand

First published by Penguin Books Australia Ltd 2003
This edition has been specially printed for the Books Alive campaign

10 9 8 7 6 5 4 3 2 1

Design by Marina Messiha, Penguin Design Studio
Cover image: 'Writing in the trenches' by J. P. Campbell;
by permission of the National Library of Australia
Illustrations by Alan Laver
Typeset in 10/15.5pt Stone Serif by Post Pre-press Group, Brisbane, Queensland
Printed and bound in Australia by McPherson's Printing Group, Maryborough, Victoria

National Library of Australia
Cataloguing-in-Publication data:

Kyle, Roy, 1897–1996.
  An Anzac's story.

  Bibliography.
  ISBN 0 14 300187 6.

  1. Kyle, Roy, 1897–1996. 2. World War, 1914–1918 – Campaigns – Turkey – Gallipoli
Peninsula – Personal narratives, Australian. I. Courtenay, Bryce, 1933– . II. Title.

940.426092

An Anzac's Story was first published with the assistance of Books Alive.

www.penguin.com.au

CONTENTS

Introduction   1

Chapter 1   The Beginning and Early Days   20
Chapter 2   Early Gooramadda Days, 1903–1909   36
Chapter 3   Germy   46
Chapter 4   Early School Days   54
Chapter 5   Notables and Others   65
Chapter 6   Family, Relatives, Pets and Fashions   69
Chapter 7   More Gooramadda Episodes   84
Chapter 8   Huckleberry Finn   88
Chapter 9   A New Beginning   96
Chapter 10   War – 1914   112
Chapter 11   Gallipoli   129
Chapter 12   After Gallipoli   196
Chapter 13   France   202
Chapter 14   Going Home   282

Family Acknowledgements   301
Bryce Courtenay's Acknowledgements   303

INTRODUCTION

Bryce Courtenay

On 4 August 1914, war was declared between Germany and England. The moment the news reached Australia, the Labor leader of the opposition and soon to be prime minister, Andrew Fisher, cabled the British Government: *'Australia is with you to the last man and the last shilling.'*

The young and the not so young fell over each other to get to the recruiting booths. Shearers in distant outback sheds put down their shears, washed their arms almost up to the elbows, rolled up their swags and headed for the nearest recruiting station. Butcher boys in the small towns and the cities wrapped up their last parcel of mutton chops, made change from a shilling, removed their aprons and headed in the same direction. Drapers rolled up their tape measures and headed for the pavement. Bank clerks completed their ledgers for the day, carefully blotted the freshly inked last line, pulled off their muslin cuff-savers, and reached for their jackets. There was a report of a Queensland drover who set off on horseback to ride the 350 miles to Brisbane and, when his horse could no longer find food in the severe drought and became too weak to continue, he abandoned it and pressed on, walking for a month along the track, living on flour from a small bag he carried and water obtained from waterholes often thirty miles apart. Rides of 2000 miles to the recruitment barracks were not uncommon and 200-mile walks to volunteer were so frequent they were seldom mentioned. Boot-makers did a roaring trade adding half an inch to the heels of young men's boots when they fell short of the five foot six inches minimum height required by the recruiting sergeant. The young men of Australia simply couldn't wait to enter the fray. The time to blood the new nation had arrived.

A popular song at the time seemed to sum up the way Australians then felt about fighting for the Mother Country:

> *For Britain! Good old Britain!*
> *Where our fathers first drew breath,*
> *We'll fight like true Australians,*
> *Facing danger, wounds or death.*
> *With Britain's other gallant sons*
> *We're going hand in hand;*

Our war-cry 'Good old Britain' boys.
Our own dear motherland.

Six years after Federation, in his book *The Real Australia*, A. J. Buchanan, a popular journalist and novelist of the time, wrote: *'Australia has so far achieved nothing great from the national standpoint. It cannot be said to have failed, because it has not yet been called upon . . . The Australian must be prepared, in the event of great emergency, to die for something or somebody.'*

The Australia in which Roy Kyle grew up has always struck me as a remarkable contradiction. We are a nation founded in misery and despair, the unwanted children of a Mother England who declared us thieves, whores and misfits and threw us out of her house, sending us to the far ends of the earth into exile where it was hoped we might be forgotten.

In 1897, the year in which Roy Kyle was born, white settlement was only in its fourth generation, and with the first two generations taking up the convict era, it is to be expected that the memories of oppression and servitude were still very much in the conscious thinking of a significant part of the various colonies. There must have been people alive whose parents were convicts and it may be postulated that they would have had no reason whatsoever to love England or to nurture in their offspring a loyalty to the King.

Yet, this seems not to have been the case. The Australians of Roy Kyle's childhood saw England as their spiritual home and regarded themselves as its true sons and daughters, willing to die for a King they had never seen and a country they had never visited. Paradoxically, this affection wasn't reciprocated. Other than accepting Australia as yet another member of an Empire upon which the sun never set, Britain did not seem to have singled out the young nation for special attention.

The enthusiasm for war among the general population was overwhelming and young men who had reached the age of eighteen, encouraged by their mothers and sweethearts, lined up, sometimes for days, outside the recruiting tents. 'For King and Country' was the popular catchcry and by 20 August, sixteen days after the declaration of war, 10,000 men had enlisted in Sydney alone. The government was offering a wage of six shillings a day to a soldier on active overseas duty. This was two shillings a day higher than the basic wage. With a major drought in progress and the consequent downturn in the economy, that extra two shillings became an added incentive to join up. The recruiting posters urged the young to 'Join the Grand Picnic in Europe' and the *Sydney Morning Herald* proclaimed that this was an opportunity for young colonials to see the Mother Country and be home shortly after Christmas. No one doubted for one moment that the stoush in Europe would be over soon and that Britain, with the help of a handful of allies and, more essentially, 'the boys from the colonies', would quickly teach the bully boy Kaiser and his upstart Germany a lesson they'd never forget. Such was the expectation of an early and easy defeat of Germany that the recruits became known as 'six-shilling tourists'.

Roy Kyle, whose memoir this is, was only sixteen when war broke out and had to wait until he was seventeen when, with his parents' permission, and stating his age as nineteen, he joined up. He remained a private throughout the war and that is why his memories are so unusual. There are hundreds of books written by high-ranking officers, historians and military experts on the Dardanelles Campaign, but few have been written by the common soldier who fought at Gallipoli and later in France.

However one such book does, in part, exist – *The Broken Years* by Bill Gammage, in which the author has collected the opinions, letters and interviews of hundreds of veterans of the Great War. I am deeply indebted to Mr Gammage and, if I single him out among the many references used, it is not to diminish the help other writers have given me but because this is the memoir of a private soldier and I have tried to keep it in context with others who shared the trenches with him, men who, like Roy Kyle, did the hard yakka and who stared down the rifle barrel at the enemy.

Roy Kyle died at the age of ninety-eight in 1996, one month

short of his ninety-ninth birthday. A friend sent me his incomplete memoir and asked if I might be interested in editing it into a book. I pointed out at the time that I was a novelist and not an academic, and that there were a great many better qualified people to undertake such a task. But I agreed, knowing that the memories of a private soldier who fought at Gallipoli should not be lost to the nation. Remarkably Roy Kyle commenced these memoirs in his eighty-ninth year and understandably his recollections are not always accurate, so I have attempted, wherever possible, to return the historical facts to his text, hopefully without disturbing the original narrative.

My additional job, as I see it, is to fill in some of the details and the background to events so that Mr Kyle's own words can be seen in their true context. While I have written on the subject of Gallipoli and France, I am not an authority on the Great War. Furthermore, in giving the reader a broader picture than Roy Kyle would have known, I will be using the only tools I have at my disposal, which are those of a storyteller. It is my experience that on the subject of war there are always experts, and I have no doubt that some of my conclusions may upset the more pedantic historians among them. In my defence, I can only claim that the myth of Gallipoli is long since established and now resides in the hearts of the men and women of our nation. Anything I say is unlikely to either enhance or change it.

It has often been said that legends are the lies nations have to have. As humans, we have a great need to believe in something bigger and more noble than the tedium of an uneventful existence. Few things in this world are wrought by logic alone, and 'interpretation' (a polite word for 'exaggeration') of even the most blatant facts is perhaps the most common habit in all of us. The making of a legend requires that an emotional element be introduced into what at the time may have been an observable truth, and the story of Gallipoli, as it has become transmuted, may be said to be the legend we had to have to become a nation in our own right.

As Australians, we are members of a young nation and there hasn't been sufficient time for us to gather too many of our own legends. Of the few we do possess, Gallipoli is the most notable and also the most paradoxical. Like the legend of Ned Kelly, by every definition a murderer and a thief who was eventually hanged for his crimes, it is a legend born out of defeat.

Gallipoli isn't even where we lost the most Australian lives. Two years later, at each of the battles of Fromelles and Pozières, there were almost the same number of casualties. It is often forgotten that three times more British and French soldiers died in the Dardanelles Campaign than Australians. Yet Gallipoli has not become one of the great British or French shrines of remembrance and is certainly not given the mythical status and deep emotional meaning it has for Australians and New Zealanders.

France and Britain are old nations who have fought too many battles and gathered too many legends for Gallipoli, an inevitable defeat born out of initial military stupidity, to count among their more notable myths.

However, for Australians and New Zealanders, it was different. Gallipoli was a first blooding away from their own soil, the testing ground for the making of a nation of warriors. It was an opportunity for our men to show they had true courage of the kind that had been romantically forged in the name of the British Empire. We were colonials bred to the stories of Rudyard Kipling and, although recently federated into a nation, we still thought of ourselves as surrogate sons of England. We needed to show the Mother Country that we were the bravest of the brave and could endure any hardship and make any sacrifice she might demand of us.

Legends of the warrior kind are most often created out of the stuff of victory, usually when the odds are greatly stacked against the final victor. They are intended to demonstrate the character and tenacity of a nation when it is threatened and they are the myths that reaffirm nationhood and instil pride and further courage into ensuing generations.

The history of England abounds in such legends: Agincourt, where a greatly outnumbered Henry V defeated France, had all the ingredients Shakespeare required for the making of a grand legend. Francis Drake's defeat of the Spanish armada was another. Nelson at Trafalgar a third. The defeat of Napoleon at Waterloo. Rorkes Drift, when a handful of Welsh Sappers met the full might of the Zulu Impi during the Zulu Wars in South Africa is yet another. The rescue of the British Expeditionary Force from Dunkirk, where Saturday sailors often in tiny single-sail family pleasure boats risked their lives to bring the tattered remains of the British Expeditionary Forces home, must surely rank as another of the grander legends of war. The London Blitz and the Battle of Britain also qualify for legendary status. The Glorious Gloucesters during the Korean War, the Battle of Goose Green in the Falklands – all were thought to be great victories against the odds that continue to create highly suitable legends to sustain the British psyche.

Australia, too, has several instances where we fought successfully against enormous odds, the battle of Long Tan in Vietnam is among the most notable. It has been claimed that eleven Victoria Crosses should have been given at Long Tan, where thirty men of 11 Platoon, D Company, 6 RAR, when caught in an ambush, successfully held off over a thousand well-trained North Vietnamese soldiers for three hours from mid-afternoon until nightfall when the enemy retreated. A cowardly Australian government, conscious that the war in Vietnam had become unpopular with the Australian people, decided against recognising their extraordinary valour and so the opportunity for another legend was lost to the nation.

Legends such as Gallipoli, which are born out of defeat, are not as easily found. Dunkirk possibly qualifies, the Charge of the Light Brigade at Balaclava certainly does and, moreover, is the nearest example Britain has to approximate the one we have acquired. The early-morning charge of the Light Brigade, an unplanned incident during the Crimean War, was all over in the late afternoon of the same day, whereas Gallipoli was a bitter struggle that took months and incorporated at least half a dozen reckless, though gloriously brave, bayonet charges that ended in disaster. Nevertheless, both share two things in common; they were brought about by a blatantly stupid and wholly misguided military decision, yet they were carried out with such supreme courage and fortitude that they've earned the right to become legends despite the fact that they met with inevitable defeat.

The war in France and Belgium was simply not suited to the making of legends. It took place over a large battle front and had become too big, too ordnance-driven and too entirely care-less of lives to acquire the credentials needed to become myths in their own right. The charnel house that was Europe in 1916, where men were routinely slaughtered in numbers too vast to imagine, was not a theatre for the high drama that makes the kinds of stories that are etched into the hearts and minds of future generations.

To this day historians argue as to whether the Great War

was necessary at all. Beyond the doubtful virtues of imperial breast-beating, there seems to have been no sound moral, religious, territorial or economic reason for it to have taken place. Germany seemed determined to go to war and had a long-standing preparation known as the Schlieffen Plan, which involved invading France, who was in alliance with Russia, in the likely event that Russia became involved.

However, an excuse was needed to get things under way and the most likely place to find one was in a quarrel taking place between Serbia and Austria. Austria was allied to Germany and when Crown Prince Franz Ferdinand of Austria was assassinated in a plot hatched by seven fanatical young Serbs acting on their own initiative, the opportunity had arrived.

Austria issued Serbia with an ultimatum and demanded an apology and recompense. Serbia, in a diplomatic panic, apologised but pointed out that they knew nothing of the plot. This was the excuse Germany needed, she could now go to the aid of Austria, who would naturally find the apology unacceptable and declare war on Serbia, with Germany as her partner in arms.

However, Serbia also had a partner in Russia, who promptly mobilised. Germany demanded that Russia demobilise or she'd declare war on her. In diplomatic terms Russia told Germany to go to hell, which was exactly what Germany had hoped she would do. Germany now had an excuse to invoke the Schlieffen Plan and to first invade France, Russia's ally.

If you're not confused at this point, there was only one further problem. In order to invade France, Germany needed to cross a neutral Belgium, who promptly refused her permission to do so. Germany, thinking Belgium to be of no consequence, decided to go ahead anyway.

During all of this foment in Europe, Britain found herself sidelined, merely an onlooker, while at the same time itching to find a way to get involved. Germany was getting much too big for her boots and Britain saw herself, the greatest imperial power in the world, about to lose her influence in Europe. She hastily dug up a treaty made in 1839, seventy-five years previously, in which she agreed to guarantee Belgium's neutrality. It was the excuse she needed and so the war to end all wars was under way.

There is a tiny footnote to all of this which has an uncomfortable parallel with today. The seven members of the plot to assassinate Crown Prince Ferdinand had all contracted tuberculosis, at that time a disease that would almost certainly kill them. In effect, the assassination was a suicide mission perpetrated by men who had nothing to lose. A seemingly meaningless decision by seven dying men that led to the deaths of a further eight million human beings.

By the time the Australians arrived in France from Gallipoli, they had already tasted the bitter fruit of defeat, and while their courage remained intact, they had largely lost their faith in British generals. The extreme winter conditions which our fighting men endured on the Somme soon disabused them of any notions of the sanctity of war. The troops had become too weary and disenchanted for any one of the endless battles to be a proving ground for valour. By the summer of 1916, when routine carnage had turned into the battles of Fromelles and Pozières, death had lost its glory and sacrifice its value.

Gallipoli was different, it was away from Europe and therefore isolated from the main event. The Turk seemed, at first, a far less romantic and worthy enemy than the German. We were a nation brought up to believe in a white Australia, and the prevailing notion at the time was that white was superior to yellow or black or brown under every circumstance and the Turk was regarded as falling somewhere within this colour bias.

The young Australian soldiers who were diverted to Egypt for further training and thereafter consigned to fight in the Dardanelles Campaign were clearly disappointed with their lot. They felt they were being allocated a lesser foe and deserved to be a part of the main game in Europe. They were anxious to be blooded by an enemy they thought worthy of their valour so they might prove themselves to be warriors of the first order.

The Australians brought an innocence into battle and this naivety was an essential ingredient in the making of the Gallipoli legend. Johnny Turk proved to be every bit a match for the young colonials. Furthermore, the propinquity of the battleground was yet another element in the grand myth to come. No commander in his right mind would have chosen to fight on such terrain, one which was clearly always going to be to the ultimate advantage of a determined enemy who commanded the heights.

Over a period of nine months, the Australian and New Zealanders failed to advance more than a few feet beyond the point they had reached on their very first day. This was an ongoing battle of yards gained and lost, of hand-to-hand bayonet fighting, where machine guns and a sniper's rifle was usually more effective than heavy artillery, and where home-made bombs and grenades made from empty jam tins became essential ordnance.

The enemy trenches were often within shouting distance, sometimes within talking distance. At one point they were two feet apart and Australian soldiers could often hear their Turkish counterparts reciting their prayers. It was a battle where each side grew to respect the other while at the same time no quarter was given and the fighting was extraordinarily savage and determined.

While the Anzacs made some attempt to bury their dead, this wasn't always possible and the dead from both sides were left lying in the sun for weeks to rot. On 6 August, the day after the battle of Lone Pine, the 8th and the 10th Light Horse regiment charged the Turkish trenches at The Nek. In less than fifteen minutes, 234 light horsemen lay dead. Most of their bodies remained there until 1919, when their sun-whitened bones were collected at last for a belated hero's burial.

The heat was merciless and the flies completely covered the corpses. And throughout was the stench, the terrible smell of rotting human flesh and excrement mixed with the sharp, acrid smell of cordite. There never seemed to be enough drinking water and in Roy Kyle's own words: *'Gallipoli was thick with lice. It didn't matter how clean you were before you entered the trenches – in ten minutes you'd be lousy.'*

It was on such a battlefield that the legend of Gallipoli was born. Where the sentiments first expressed by Buchanan in 1907, were resolved.

Gallipoli was where the very first blooding of the nation took place and where our young men left the battlefield defeated in what had become a stalemate, but without surrendering to the enemy, so that their honour and pride was said to have remained intact and they had lived to fight another day. The same must be said of the New Zealanders who fought with fierce resolve and equal passion and distinction at Gallipoli. It is surprising that after the horror and hardship of Gallipoli a general disillusion with war wasn't present. The men who left the trenches at Gallipoli still believed in the righteousness of England's war against Germany.

In 1916 an Australian private, who found himself about to enter the war in Europe, wrote in his notebook:

Here's to the Kaiser, the son of a bitch,
May his balls drop off with the seven-year itch,
May his arse be pounded with a lump of leather,
Till his arsehole can whistle 'Britannia forever.'

It was the war on the Somme that finally forced us to re-evaluate the blind allegiance we had previously felt for the Mother Country. As the Australians became involved in a war that seemed to have no remission, having fought in the frozen mire of the European winter, the mud and slush of the spring offensive and the summer dust and heat of battle, they were now well and truly blooded and no longer wide-eyed and bushy-tailed. Back home, we were beginning to see this protracted war for what it was: essentially the grandstanding of two imperious and vainglorious nations both calling on their every alliance to win a meaningless contest.

Moreover, while it could only be said in whispers, we began to see England, the once cherished Mother Country, for what she had become – a mother essentially preoccupied with herself, careless to a fault with the lives of her native sons and even less caring of the fate of those from her colonies.

As the wounded began to return and the daily published lists of the dead grew ever longer, the euphoria was over and doubt took its place. Wilfred Owen, the great English war poet killed on the last day before armistice, wrote a poem that best sums up the sentiments Australian mothers and their English counterparts were increasingly coming to possess:

Arms and the Boy

Let the boy try along this bayonet-blade
How cold steel is, and keen with hunger of blood;
Blue with all malice, like a madman's flash;
And thinly drawn with famishing for flesh.

Lend him to stroke these blind, blunt bullet-leads,
Which long to nuzzle in the hearts of lads,
Or give him cartridges whose fine zinc teeth
Are sharp with sharpness of grief and death.

For his teeth seem for laughing round an apple.
There lurk no claws behind his fingers supple;
And God will grow no talons at his heels,
Nor antlers through the thickness of his curls.

And so, in 1918 the war to end all wars ground to a halt with more than eight and a half million dead on both sides and at least a further twenty-one million wounded. The price had been too high for what proved to be a largely empty prize, a pyrrhic victory that had exhausted Europe and undermined the structure of the British Empire by sending England broke.

We buried our dead and looked into the exhausted and troubled eyes of the wounded and those of the battle-weary young men who returned to our shores outwardly unscathed, and we saw that they had become changed in spirit forever. In Roy Kyle's own words: *'War really changed a person. Soldiers who went over came back different men.'*

As a people, we now knew with certainty that we were no longer the trusting colonial sons and daughters of England. Henceforth we would stand on our own feet, weigh the arguments proposed by others, and make our own decisions to get involved. Andrew Fisher's unequivocal promise to Britain of support, to the last man and the last shilling, had become a quaint sentiment belonging to a different time and it had no place in the notions of a nation which now began to regard itself as separate and independent.

In 1901, when the various colonies within Australia federated and a new nation was proclaimed, most of its citizens were still emotionally attached to their antecedent homeland. The antipodean-born Irish remained fiercely Irish and Catholic, and the remaining population, for the most part Protestant, saw England, Scotland or Wales as their Mother Country. Australia was an accident of birth and their hearts and emotions lay elsewhere. The puppet strings were finally cut when the Great War eventually came to an end. For the first time we began to see ourselves emotionally as a united and unique people who proudly called themselves Australians. The sense of being a different people, which began at Gallipoli, passed through disillusion and despair and ended in a knowledge and confidence that we could control our own destiny as a free and independent nation.

At the very moment that first Turkish rifle shot ricocheted off a pebble on Anzac beach, the colonial mantle fell from our shoulders and the men who charged the steep rise leading up from the beach were in their hearts and minds Australians at war. Within the whine and clatter of gunfire and in the chaos that followed the pre-dawn stillness, our nation's first great legend was about to be born.

CHAPTER 1

The Beginning and Early Days

Over the years, members of my family have, from time to time, suggested that I record my recollections of events in my life. This is not because my life has been in any way unusual. It has, in fact, been very much a 'run of the mill' life except for four horrific years in the First World War and because it has spanned almost two-thirds of the period of white settlement in Victoria and almost forty-four per cent of the period since the arrival of Governor Phillip and the First Fleet at Botany Bay.

Unfortunately, I have been overdue in commencing the task, and now, in my eighty-ninth year, my memory has diminished and the flow of words has considerably dried up. The delay is my own fault entirely and is due mainly to the fear of appearing obsessively absorbed in myself. However, if my recollections are to see the light of day,

I must face up to it, and trust the personal pronoun 'I' will not appear too frequently.

———◆———

As a writer it is my ardent hope that at the age of eighty-nine I am as clear thinking and articulate as Roy Kyle when, at that age, he commenced to write this memoir. It is claimed that, as you grow older, the early part of your memory returns and the part that remembers whether you need a carton of milk loves to play hide and seek.

Though I often forget to buy milk, I can clearly remember when a billy can was left at the front doorstep to await the early-morning arrival of the milko in his horse and cart. He would scoop your order into it from a large milk can of the kind you now see propped on its side and raised on a short pipe set into cement to be used as a letterbox on rural properties of pretension.

I recall when only the doctor could afford a fridge and the ice chest was just coming into fashion, with most working-class homes still using the Coolgardie or meat safe placed in a convenient spot to catch the breeze. Those homes with an ice chest would know that the ice never quite lasted until the ice man returned with another block and how, when he did, he would chip a tiny translucent sliver off the corners for the kids to suck.

Several years ago, while doing research for one of my

books, I had occasion to interview a ninety-six-year-old lady, who must have been born around the same time as Roy Kyle and who had spent her life in a small town in northern New South Wales. 'What are the inventions in the twentieth century you think were the most important?' I asked.

'Oh, that's easy,' she replied. 'Fly screens and elastic for bloomers.'

It is hardly possible, in these days of electronic gadgets where it is claimed that the average home has sufficient labour-saving devices to replace the work of eight servants in an upper-class Victorian home, to imagine what Australia was like in Roy Kyle's childhood.

In just over one hundred years, almost everything has changed. When Roy Kyle was born, two out of three Australian colonials lived in rural areas. Today the situation is almost exactly reversed. A hundred years ago, ninety-five per cent of the population of 3.8 million was British and ninety-nine per cent were white, with a smattering of Chinese, Afghans and Pacific Islanders, always remembering that the Indigenous people were not included in the census. Today, Australia's twenty-one million people form one of the most polyglot nations on earth, with every colour and creed represented.

The Australian character of today would be hard to pin down and any description would be forced to resort to generalities. Not so at the turn of the century. Here is how the *Commonwealth Year Book of 1909* describes us: '*The Australian at present is little more than a transplanted Briton, with the essential characteristics of his forebears, the desire for freedom from restraint, however, being more strongly accentuated.*'

Portions of the nation's diet are still to be found in some rural areas and even within some older suburbs where Sunday dinner (lunch) after church is still a tradition with its ubiquitous roast lamb or beef and gravy, roast potatoes and pumpkin, though, even in rural areas, our diet has changed considerably. In Roy Kyle's time the household fare was based on a somewhat monotonous British middle-class cold-climate diet. This consisted mainly of meat, bread, potatoes and tea, supplemented by milk and eggs, with the main fresh vegies pumpkin and cabbage, both easy to grow in the harsh climate. The meat was much as it is today, steak, lamb chops or sausages, but to this was commonly added corned beef and boiled mutton. Alas, today boiled mutton is a rarity.

The Australian soldiers in the A.I.F. were taller and stronger than their English counterparts and this was mainly due to sport in the open air and a greater intake of protein. In 1906 Australians ate 264 pounds (approx. 119 kg) of beef per head per year whereas the amount for an

Englishman was 100 pounds (45 kg). The French con-
sumed 85 pounds (38 kg) and the German diet consisted
of just 64 pounds (29 kg). Meat was said to be served
three times a day in Australian homes.

Interestingly, in Mrs Beeton's famous cookbook, the
mainstay of the British middle-class kitchen, there were
recipes for kangaroo-tail soup, parrot pie and roast wal-
laby. With perhaps the exception of the odd bushman
dependent on game, the rabbit shooter thoroughly sick of
bunny stew and the swaggie down on his luck, Australians
didn't care much for indigenous protein. It is also curious
that with fish potentially plentiful as a source of protein,
it was only eaten on Fridays by Catholics and even then
was mostly of a smoked variety such as haddock.

No radio network existed and a telephone in a home was
a very rare occurrence indeed, although the new telegraph
service was just coming into play. Country newspapers, at
the cost of a penny, were the vital source of news and information. They informed country people of mail closing and
arrival times, river steamboat and train services, notices of
parcels arriving by train, forthcoming visits by dentists,
chiropodists and, in the more remote parts, the doctor or
district nurse or even the circuit magistrate. The social
columns were considered very important, as gossip, local
and from the city, was an essential part of life in the bush

and, of course, they included the news from England, with other international news taking a minor role.

School was compulsory for children aged between six and fourteen when most left in Form Three, usually their fourteenth year. Secondary school was not available in the country. In the Victoria of Roy Kyle's time, the only state secondary schools were in Melbourne, Ballarat and Bendigo. Teaching was stereotyped and children learned mainly by rote, with their memories greatly enhanced by the liberal use of the cane. Teachers were, for the most part, inadequately trained and poorly paid, with most country classrooms containing multiple streams.

Dual loyalty was emphasised in government schools, and patriotism was concerned with both one's country and the British Empire. At least a quarter of the songs taught in schools were on British patriotic themes. In 1905, when Roy Kyle would have been at school, Empire Day was instituted for the sole purpose of celebrating Britain's far-flung conquests. Empire Day was declared a school holiday, with bags of free lollies handed out to the kids. The day was filled with stirring oratory, brass bands, marching, cheering and much flapping of Union Jacks supplied for the occasion. Every schoolchild was taught that the red parts on the map of the world 'belong to us' and that to be British was a privileged state of being.

Loyalty to King and Country and the concept of England as the Mother Country had been inculcated almost in the cradle. At school, pupils learned the history of both Australia and England, with the emphasis being that our own history was of little consequence while that of England was about the continuity of a people and therefore of primary importance. It should be remembered that at that time the convict era was looked upon with great shame and families with transported ancestors were careful to conceal the circumstances that had brought their forebears to the burning shores.

In 1911, just four years before war was declared, there were only 3896 cars registered in New South Wales, with a little more than twice that number in the whole of Australia. The Wright brothers had made their first flight in the Kittyhawk just eight years earlier and it was not until 1917 that Australia possessed two aeroplanes, which they used to rather grandly form the Royal Australian Flying Corps. The horse was still the most common means for travelling any distance locally and the buggy was used for the family, though many of the poorer families walked. It was not unusual for people never to have visited the town twenty miles down the road. In the cities, folk caught a tram of one of four types – steam, electricity, cable or horse-driven – while seriously long-distance travel was by riverboat or train.

When Kyle was still a small child, the country areas were recovering from a depression that had seen many of the banks collapse. This was compounded by a rabbit plague and the most severe drought on record, which lasted from 1895 to 1905. Many of the poorer families subsisted on bread and boiled rabbit, which had to be boiled because the flesh contained not an ounce of fat. Homemade pie-melon jam was the only confection they could afford.

The depression produced swagmen, shearers, casual bush workers and prospectors in large numbers, who, by moving about, were just about able to get by, though making enough to eat each day was always a serious concern. Many of the men who volunteered for the A.I.F. did not do so out of loyalty to King and Country, they came from families still recovering from the depression and the army wage was considered a fortune to men who were often hard put to earn sixpence for a day's work. Six shillings a day was enough to keep their families in a manner beyond their wildest dreams. Enough even for a soldier boy to enjoy an occasional bottle of beer with his mates and to buy a tin of Champion Flake, the preferred tobacco of the day.

Kyle remembers his childhood with great fondness, but for most country people these were hard times and he was fortunate that his father was employed as a border customs officer, a job that ensured some safety in difficult times.

These inland custom posts existed because some of the colonies chose to protect their industries with tariffs, while others preferred free trade. A customs bureau existed on the borders of the various colonies and duty needed to be paid on goods 'imported' from one colony to another.

It was not a system much liked by anyone and the customs officer and the local policeman posted on the border were often led a merry dance. Farmers would commonly swim their stock over quiet stretches of river to avoid tax, or smuggle them along bush tracks at night. Goods tended to be cheaper in New South Wales so Victorians would cross the river to buy their clothes and groceries, and women, often wearing several layers of clothing, would pass through customs on the way home. Like most bureaucratic decisions, customs duties were inconsistent and lacked commonsense. As an example of this, flour and bread were taxed in Victoria but dough was not, so bakers set up dough houses across the border in New South Wales and ferried their dough back across the river on the early-morning ferry, to be baked into bread on the Victorian side.

The system was proving more of a nuisance than a major source of revenue to those colonies protecting their industries and, towards the end of the nineteenth century, the demand for 'free trade' was a popular catchcry and one that was to become one of the earliest motivational forces for Federation. The system of independent colonies was proving to be unworkable, railways were being built with different gauges, telegraph and postal systems weren't compatible and made communication between the various colonies very difficult. It also didn't help that every colony used a different currency.

However, there was one more compelling emotional reason for Federation, the defence of the whole of the country against the fear of the Asian hordes. It was believed that the 'Yellow Peril' was poised and ready to cross the seas to swamp the white man and his precious way of life. The seeds of the White Australia Policy, sown during the riots against Chinese miners in the goldfields in the 1860s, was to be finally harvested with the advent of Federation.

In terms of defence, Roy Kyle would have been a compulsory cadet. This was how Australian boys were prepared in both body and mind for the Great War of 1914–18. Voluntary school cadet corps had existed in most of the colonies since the 1870s, but, at the urging of Lord Kitchener, who visited Australia after the Boer War, these were replaced with various forms of compulsory training.

The system was greatly disliked by the working-class youths, who deeply resented having to give up the only free afternoon they were given in a working week to go to drill training. The children of the rich, most of whom were still at school, did their training during school hours. This would have been the case with Roy Kyle, who, while not from a wealthy family, had moved with his family to Ballarat and obtained a scholarship to a private school.

The cadet system was seen by the government as more than just a preparation for war; it was also designed, or so people thought, to keep fourteen-year-old school leavers, who were reaching puberty with its attendant problems, from causing trouble and it was believed to be an excellent way to discipline and prepare wayward and excitable and, therefore troublesome, young men for tedious and mindless work in modern factories.

Over 6000 'boys' were gaoled over four years for failing to turn up to drill. A typical case was that of David William Fitzgerald, a fourteen-year-old who was 44½ hours in arrears with his drills. Brought before the stipendiary magistrate, he pleaded that he worked from daylight until dark and lived nearly five miles out of town and had no horse to bring him in and, besides, as a manual worker he was too exhausted at the end of the day to drill. The stipendiary magistrate brushed his plea aside. 'If there was a football match on, you would soon walk in,' he declared, sentencing the boy to a £5 fine (ten dollars), which amounted to six months' wages, a fortune a poor boy couldn't hope to pay, and to which was added a further fifteen shillings in court costs or, if he was unable to pay, six weeks in the reformatory.

However, for those privileged to continue school, the cadet system was seen as teaching obedience, respect, self-control, mental alertness and responsibility. In addition, the secondary-school system recognised such pupils as officers in a future army and so the drill was augmented with lessons on the dignity of manhood, the virtue of womanhood, the innocence of childhood, the importance of Empire and the guarding of their country's flag, which, at the time, had only recently had five stars added to the all-embracing Union Jack.

In true tradition, war was seen as a game where sportsmanship and true manliness was tested. It was what made the British brave, fair-minded, resourceful and compassionate. Winning wasn't in question, it was how you won that mattered, and if you were born with a white skin and were at the same time privileged to be a member of the British Empire, you won because you possessed superior values, partook of and were well trained in sport, and knew how to defeat an opponent with skill, intelligence and daring. At the conclusion of the Great War, when such notions had long since been forsaken on the battlefield and, where nearly a million fair-minded, sporting, blue-eyed Englishmen lay buried in the mud of the

Somme, a speech made in the English parliament declared to a convocation of misty-eyed old men in celluloid collars and top hats that Germany's defeat was due to 'the greatest game our race has ever played'.

It must have been highly effective propaganda. Over 300,000 Australians educated under this system volunteered to fight the Empire's wars. Moreover, school teachers were prominent on the recruitment lists. Of the 1500 male school teachers in Victoria aged between eighteen and forty-five, more than half joined up. The proportion for the other states was similar. Roy Kyle was a typical example of the middle-class youth of the times. At seventeen he had been mentally and spiritually prepared for the war and apparently quite easily succeeded in persuading his parents that it was time for him to fight for King, Country and an Empire upon which the sun, it was claimed, never set.

The story of Private Roy Kyle begins.

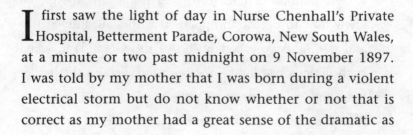

I first saw the light of day in Nurse Chenhall's Private Hospital, Betterment Parade, Corowa, New South Wales, at a minute or two past midnight on 9 November 1897. I was told by my mother that I was born during a violent electrical storm but do not know whether or not that is correct as my mother had a great sense of the dramatic as did most of her brothers and sisters, many of whom believed, on what evidence I do not know, that they were descended from the great Welsh actress Sarah Siddons (1755–1831). I was the third in the family, my brother Leonard (Len) and sister Muriel (Birdie) having preceded me by seven and five years respectively. Marjorie followed ten years after me.

I have no recollection of my life in Corowa, so anything I say about it is from what my parents told me and what I picked up from family conversations. Fortunately, my memory remains very good on things I heard and saw in years long past, although very faulty for the happenings of yesterday.

At the time of my birth my father occupied and worked a dairy farm named 'Riverside', a short distance from Corowa, which he held on lease from Mr F. C. Piggin, a stock and station agent of that town. Before that, he had worked in the drapery business, with a period as a jackaroo on Moira Station in NSW, and he had resigned as departmental manager of the Benalla branch of Millers Stores of Geelong to begin dairy farming at Corowa. After a succession of droughts, he had to surrender his lease. Then he started a butchering business in Corowa, which was apparently unsuccessful, and about late 1899 or early 1900 he obtained a position with H. Garrison, General Merchant, of Camperdown.

After two years with Garrisons he transferred to F. Oakley and Co., but left Camperdown in June 1903 to take up duties as a stock inspector with the Department of Agriculture. The family moved temporarily to Geelong, while Father took charge of the supervision of an outbreak of anthrax at Dookie Agricultural College. After about six months, when the outbreak had been defeated, he was posted as Inspector of Stock and Collector of Customs at the Gooramadda–Howlong crossing of the Murray River.

During our stay in Geelong we three children – Len, Birdie and I – contracted the then dreaded disease diphtheria. We were patients in the Geelong Public Hospital. Len and Birdie were soon discharged after treatment with the newly discovered antitoxin that was instrumental in banishing the great fear of diphtheria throughout the civilised world. I was more seriously affected and remained in hospital for some time longer.

During my stay in hospital an event occurred, which my mother would tell with great effect for a long time afterwards. One night, a nurse went to check up on my bed and – in one of Mother's long dramatic pauses – discovered it was empty! I was found in the hospital garden, delirious, with a very high temperature, and very cold. I survived, but returned home to promptly fall off the edge of a packing case, in which I was trying to imitate a tightrope walker recently seen at the Fitzgerald Brothers' Circus. I inflicted a four- or five-inch cut on the top of my head by contact with a corner upright in the unlined washhouse, where the case was being packed in anticipation of our move to Gooramadda and the beginning of a new era in our lives. That is, in the lives of my parents, my sister and myself. My brother, Len, was being left behind in Geelong to attend the Flinders State School, which was diagonally across La

Trobe Terrace from the home of my paternal grandparents, with whom he lived in a fine old Georgian-type home on the corner of Elizabeth Street (now Roebuck Street). It remains today as sound as the day it was built over a hundred years ago.

CHAPTER 2

Early Gooramadda Days, 1903–09
Mainly Snakes, Sheep and Playmates

You will not find Gooramadda on maps other than those large enough to carry the names of areas as distinct from villages. Its one and only claim to inclusion in any map is that it is at the end of the road on the Victorian side of the Murray River and a bridge leading to the small NSW town of Howlong, one mile distant, which is about midway between Albury and Corowa. Apart from the river crossing, its only claim to recognition is that it was the highest point up the river reached by a Murray paddleboat.

Anyone reading this book may wonder why an inspector of stock and a customs officer was required at a river crossing connecting Victoria and New South Wales between 1903 and 1909. Let me explain.

The year was 1903. Federation of the Australian States into the Commonwealth of Australia had been proclaimed on 1 January 1901 . . . Before Federation, each state had the status of a separate colony and, in fact, if not entirely in practice, was a foreign country to the others. Accordingly, customs duties were payable for the passage of goods and livestock from one state to another. Following Federation, this practice gradually disappeared but, for stock, it was still in operation in 1903 and, indeed, for some years after.

At the Victorian end of the bridge was a race through which all stock were diverted to a river flat, between our house and the river. Father would stand at the entrance to the race so he could run his eye over every animal passing down it, pressing a lever on the little adding machine he held in the palm of his hand as each animal headed down the race. Any animal whose condition he felt dissatisfied with, he would divert through a side gate into a fenced yard for a thorough inspection later. The largest number of sheep I remember was a mob of ten thousand and it must have been a tiring job standing on the side of a dusty road with the drovers yelling, their whips cracking, the dogs barking and thousands of sheep struggling to get through an entrance made for one, particularly if it was a hot day, which it always was when large mobs were on the move.

After the mob was on the river flat, where they invariably stayed for the night guarded by dogs, the boss drover would report to Father's office by the side of our house, about a hundred yards from the bridge, to settle the account. How this was done I do not know as I have no recollection of any quantity of cash, although there was a small safe in the office. The payment was probably made by cheque or an order on the owner that was sent by coach in a small sealed mailbag to catch the train at Chiltern, there being no railway at Howlong. Its destination was the Department of Agriculture in Melbourne.

Father was a non-drinker and detested all intoxicating drink so the poor drover would have to quench his thirst with a cup of tea until he was free to make a dash to Rutzou's Punt Hotel two or three hundred yards up the road . . .

There was normally a bonus for me after the crossing of a large mob of sheep from NSW, particularly in the lambing season when, in the hollows of trees and logs and underneath logs lying over a depression in the ground, I would find a young lamb or two. Sometimes a drover would give me one which was too weak to travel any further. My sister and I would feed the lambs on milk from a baby's bottle – of which we always had a plentiful supply – and take good care of them until they were strong enough to fend for themselves, when they would go in the rich river flat of our twenty-acre paddock.

The largest number of lambs I ever had at any one time was fifteen. When they began to disappear, one or two at a time, I knew they had been sold to the local butcher, especially after lamb would appear on the dinner table. That was always too much for me and I would flee the table to my bedroom, where my sister would soon follow to comfort me until my tears dried up. I do not know who got the money for the lambs – undoubtedly Mother or Father – nor did I care as I did not want any of it. It may have paid the butcher's bill. As a variation, Mother once brought me a piglet, which was given the name Emma. With a diet mainly of milk and bran and grain, Emma grew into a fine specimen and became quite a pet. Mother eventually tired of footing the cost of feeding, which she estimated at five shillings per week (quite a sum in 1905), so Emma was sold to the butcher for thirty shillings. To add insult to injury, roast pork was on the table the following Sunday. I took the well-worn track to my bedroom.

Our house was commodious enough, of weatherboard construction, but riddled with white ants. I would be in bed at night and actually hear them on the other side of the wallpaper. When we moved to Ballarat, we discovered that most of the picture frames had been eaten out, and all that was left was the varnish.

The white ants worried me, and no doubt frightened me greatly, but I don't remember ever complaining about them: knowing, I suppose, full well that nothing could be done about it. My father complained to his superiors but they, comfortably installed in Melbourne, would not or could not do anything to eradicate the pests. None of Father's colleagues, to my knowledge, ever visited the place, so they would have no idea of the conditions. For many years, in fact, until my late teens, I had recurrent nightmares in which I dreamed that my legs were eaten by the termites. I would wake in terror and lie in a cold sweat until the fear disappeared. Winter was the worst time: in summer we slept on the verandah, which was on two sides of the house, and the main enemy there were the mosquitoes, but more about that later.

Our only neighbours were the Rutzous, who occupied and conducted the hotel (shanty would better describe it) up the road. The building was a ramshackle place of weatherboard and iron, and in the hot weather the heat in the minuscule little bar must have been insufferable and brought about unquenchable thirsts that could not be satisfied with beer drawn from an unprotected cask. Occasionally as I passed the open bar door on tip-toe, I glimpsed the great head and torso of Mr Rutzou behind the bar, where he sat immobile. He was, I think, a kindly, perhaps gentle, man but I never got close enough to him to find out. Our fear of him was due to his appearance. To us, he seemed to have the head and the body of a giant and the legs of a dwarf. We were told by his children that he had been left out in his pram in the sun as a baby and that the sun had shrivelled his legs. A most unlikely story that did nothing to abate our terror. By 'our' I mean my sister and I. He reminded us very forcibly of Rumpelstiltskin of Grimms' fairy tales, with which we were familiar.

The shanty was an unsavoury place and it was widely believed that many men who 'had too many' were 'persuaded' to stay until their cash ran out.

Mrs Rutzou was a slight, dark woman. She kept her children spotlessly clean. They were, in addition, well behaved and I remember them as clean in mind and behaviour. They were Roman Catholics but Mother gradually accepted that they were acceptable playmates, provided I did not go near the pub.

The next nearest family were the Costains, who lived in an

unfloored slab-and-bark hut about a mile away through heavily timbered country. There were numerous Costain children, all as wild as March hares, and their numbers increased by one a year. We always knew when a new one was arriving as Father, who had a considerable knowledge of animals, became the recognised accoucheur for the district and would go off in the middle of the night, dressed in his Sunday suit and carrying his little black bag, which usually contained various stock medicines that presumably were replaced by antiseptics such as carbolic and lysol on such occasions. Usually, a pair of chickens or, if times were bad, a pair of rabbits would be delivered at the house a day or two later by a bashful bare-footed Costain boy who would hand them over and dash to the cover of the scrub. The prevalent rumour was that Father had done part of a medical course, which he had abandoned just prior to completion to become a stock inspector. A likely story! Because of this reputation, he administered to other ailments of the Costains and their likes, most of whom lived a little further away and in better circumstances in as much as their floors were covered.

Father Costain supported his brood by rabbit trapping, and working on the roads and the vineyards, there being plenty of the latter nearby. His family lived in conditions which the modern adult or child would find hard to realise.

I only once glimpsed the interior of their hut, which was in a small clearing in the scrub. The hut appeared to be of two rooms, with all the children sleeping in one room, the parents in the other. Around this room were several beds or bunks, each consisting of hessian drawn over four stakes driven into the ground, and on each of the beds was a very threadbare grey blanket. The younger children presumably slept on the blankets that were tossed in heaps on the ground. The table was like the beds, a homemade affair and was surrounded by rough, backless benches.

Most of the eating was done outside where a bush oven was surrounded by logs and tin eating vessels were scattered on a rough table. Several dogs snoozed in the sun, and the fowls that scratched around the area probably, from the looks of it, ventured inside sometimes . . .

For some long-forgotten reason there was a deadly feud between one of the Costain boys and myself. Whenever we met, it was a point of honour that we exchanged a few blows in passing. I don't think we ever hurt each other but, from our wild screaming and hideous grimaces, we certainly tried to frighten each other. One encounter was more serious and could have easily led to disaster. Our cow was dry and I was on my way to collect milk from the people who had a neat little property perhaps half a mile beyond Costains. I had to cross a creek which was usually dry but was now a raging torrent. The only way across was over a fallen log, along which was some fencing wire, about two feet above the log, to hang on to in case of a slip. As luck would have it, we met in mid-stream and as neither of us would give way, we each hung on to the wire with one hand (I was rather handicapped by having also to hang on to a billy can full of milk) and punched with the other. Neither of us would give way until, after a few slips on the log, we decided that honour had been served, and squeezed past each other to go our separate ways. Our animosity cooled after that, although for several months we continued to take passing swipes at each other, but they lacked the purpose of former times. We had learned, at least partially, the meaning of compromise.

A word about the Rutzou children. There were three of them. I have but a hazy recollection of the eldest, who was named Vern. I do not know why my memory of him is so clouded as I do remember that he took part in all our games. The next one down was Trevor – Trev for short – who was about my own age, and the youngest was Gloria, a dear little girl who tried valiantly to keep up with us but was always the whipper-in. She was, I remember, always spotlessly turned out in a starched white pinafore and with a bow in her hair. As pretty as paint and as gentle as a doe. I wonder what became of her? We were always very solicitous for her although after an afternoon of yabbying, frog catching and sometimes fishing, her pristine appearance would be badly soiled. She would nevertheless turn up spotless the next day. We had many a happy time with a snow-white pony lent to us by Mr McVean, the local squatter of Howlong Station; the pony was a nuggety little thing without any vices.

Father and Mr McVean had become friendly, brought about I imagine by Father's knowledge of stock and their membership of the same church. The McVean children had learnt to ride on the pony but had outgrown it. The pony had a growth the size of a cricket ball under its tail, which Father always itched to remove but he was restrained by fear of what he might find. The three of us, Trev and I bare-footed, Gloria with highly polished shoes, used to mount Snowy – one on its withers, Gloria in the middle, and one on its rump – and ride it around the paddock. I think the pony enjoyed it as much as we did.

One day I had a nasty experience with Snowy. I had formed the habit when on my own of putting him at every log I came across, and they were numerous. This day I put him at one larger than usual and he baulked and we parted company. I executed a parabola over the log and directly below me was a sharp-pointed broken-off stump of sapling. I missed it by a convulsive twist of my body. Lesson two: never jump anything unless you know what is on the land-ing side.

But I ignored the lesson because a few months later I jumped off the same log, barefooted as usual, and directly below me was a coiled-up snake enjoying the sun. Another convulsive twist and I was away before the snake could uncoil itself quickly enough to strike. That time I was really scared and the lesson sunk in.

The area was alive with snakes although we seldom saw them, but their tracks across the dusty roads were numer-ous, especially on the first half of the mile-long road to Howlong, where there were two bridges – one over the river and one over a lagoon and a number of culverts. These were buttressed at both ends by piled rocks, amongst which the snakes had their abode. A famous snake charmer named Morrisy – later killed in South Africa by a snake bite during an exhibition – caught twenty in this area in one afternoon.

The following day he was charged in Albury with being a vagrant and, when asked by the police magistrate what he had in the sack he was carrying, emptied the twenty snakes out onto the courtroom floor, which cleared the room in record time.

There was a culvert, or rather a short bridge, between our house and the bridge over the river, which housed an over-sized snake. We never saw the snake but Father measured its track in the dust at 10½ inches. The only person who saw it, to our knowledge, was a woman who used to come from Howlong once a week to help Mother with the washing. She arrived one Monday morning (Monday being washing day) in a state of collapse after seeing the snake cross the road in front of her. Her startled imagination saw it as some prehistoric reptile, but there is no doubt the snake was large . . .

CHAPTER 3

Germy

This lovable old German fisherman played a large part in the lives of all of us and deserves a chapter on his own.

When we first came to Gooramadda he was camped on the riverbank on the NSW side with another old German known only to us, and I expect to Germy, as Charlie. We didn't know them and never did get to know Charlie as some short time after our arrival, they fell out and Charlie took his departure and was never heard of again . . .

After the departure of Charlie, Germy asked permission to camp on our land and, permission being granted, erected his tent on the riverbank about 200 yards from our house, where he stayed with short breaks until we left some six years later.

We loved the old chap and I'm sure he loved us. It was probably the one and only time he had known love and warmth since leaving his native Germany as a young man, and he repaid it with a loyalty which had to be experienced to be believed. Germy had his difficult side, when he would refuse any reward or payment for work done, and he did plenty. He felled trees, sawed logs, and split and stacked them for our stove and open fires. We always had several cords neatly stacked and ready for the fire, all carried some hundreds of yards to the house.

I spent many carefree hours at Germy's camp and, although there must have been times when I annoyed him, he never showed it nor did he ever speak angrily to me. He gave me lots of good advice though never couched as advice, and taught me a lot about the bush and its inhabitants. He also, after much pleading, would sometimes roll me a cigarette with tobacco cut from a black plug rolled to small pieces in his hands, and then rolled into what firstly resembled a cigarette in a piece of newspaper or, if that was not available, in a piece of some grocery wrapping. Having lit it from a coal from the fire, I would stretch out on Germy's bunk and let my childish imagination run riot. One day I would be a gallant British soldier cutting down enemies disdainfully in defence of King and Empire, the next a hunter (British, of course) in the wilds of Africa, just as nonchalantly destroying lions and tigers . . .

Fortunately, the cigarette would soon go out or disintegrate, having been stuck together with spit, before I became sick from it.

The modern child could not understand such mental play-acting any more than he could understand the great pride in being part of the great British Empire 'on which the sun never set' and which was shown on maps in red splashes covering about one-third of the world. Then there was the All Red Route shown as thin red lines linking the numerous colonies, possessions and protectorates and other trading nations to the British Isles; all dominated and protected by the British fleet. There was the British Raj in India, dominated by the gallant British army controlling (all for their own good, mind you) many hundreds of millions of heathen Indians. Sometimes, the ungrateful Indians did not see it our way, particularly the turbaned Sikhs to the north-west, but they were soon taught a lesson, albeit with the loss of a number of brave British Red Coats who, in the popular jargon of the day, 'died willingly for their King and country'.

Fortunately, those days are gone, but it took two ghastly world wars to destroy them. May they never return.

But to get back to Germy. I never heard him swear or say anything that he would not say before my mother or Birdie. One of his self-imposed chores was to stand by the noticeboard outside Father's office, with its collection of crested notices pinned on it and, in answer to the question from illiterate passers-by as to 'what place is this?', he would reply with great conviction, 'This is the police station.' They would probably have suspected it from the official-looking notices, whose like they had seen in many a police station, and would promptly head for the bridge and New South Wales.

Germy caught fish mainly on night lines, which were prohibited, but nobody took any notice of that, the nearest policeman on the Victorian side being thirteen miles away at Rutherglen. Although Howlong on the NSW side had a mounted policeman, he had a wide area to cover and little time, or inclination, to devote to seeking out night lines, which in any case were always skilfully hidden. The small fish – mainly cod – Germy would give to Mother; the larger ones he would sell in Howlong to the Hamilton Brothers' general store, the hotels – there were two – or the butcher. He would also do a little rabbit trapping, and thus eke out an existence until shearing time came around.

Each year, from memory, but I am not now sure of the exact time (it was in early spring), Germy would arrive at the house early one morning to say goodbye before setting out on his annual pilgrimage to a few sheep stations where he acted as shearers' cook and roustabout. He would have his swag on his shoulder and his billy can in his hand, and I never ceased to be amazed at the numerous items packed in the latter. Visible would be packets of flour, sugar and tea, and a plug or two of black tobacco, fishing gear . . . In his bowyangs would be a knife, fork and spoon. We never knew for certain the location or the names of the stations he went to but they were understood to be hundreds of miles away. One was I think Briagolong, between Khancoban and Corryong.

Just before Christmas Germy would return decked out in his new togs – corduroy trousers, black boots, blue shirt, blue serge jacket and stiff-brimmed felt hat, and glory of glories, a new half-crown watch which was good for at least a few months. Mother always insisted on him sitting down to a meal. He invariably arrived out of meal times, so he had it on his own. After a meal, he would leave for his camp and soon a thin column of smoke would signal that normality had returned. Such was Germy's independence that always a florin (two shilling piece) would be found under his plate. Instances of his extreme independence are too numerous to record. Another one will suffice. It was on Christmas Day, 1903 – his first on our land – and Mother sent me down to him with a plate of poultry and vegetables and a small pudding she had cooked for him. He refused to accept the food on the grounds that he had not earned it and that he had no money to pay for it. Father then took it down, with the same result. Silly, undoubtedly, but that was Germy – give everything and accept nothing.

During his absence, the care of his camp would be in my hands, and it was the only time that the fire in front of his tent would go out. The camp and fire were on river sand with the fire enclosed on three sides by sheets of iron. Many the feast I have had by that fire; always fresh damper and jam, often a potato roasted in its skin, and fish baked on hot flat stones and covered with red-hot coals. All washed down with a tin mug full of black billy tea plentifully laced with sugar. After washing up in the river, there would be a snooze on the sand or under a tree if it was hot, or in the tent if it was cold. This is really the only way to cook fish. However, it may be just as well to seek advice from a Germy beforehand. The stones, by the way, were in a hole several inches deep in the sand.

The biggest fish I saw Germy catch was a thirty-pound

cod, and this was on a hand line a few yards from his tent, although he told me he had once caught a sixty-pounder on a night line up near Corryong before moving to Gooramadda. He had made thirty shillings by cutting the sixty-pounder into steaks and hawking them from door to door in the town.

Sitting by his fire one day, Germy became reminiscent for the one and only time and told me how he had come to Australia. This is his story:

As a youth of eighteen he had been called upon for service in the German navy and had to report at Kiel for examination. The navy was the last service he wanted to enter so he signed on as member of the crew of a sailing ship out of Hamburg. He explained that there were so many young men being conscripted into the rapidly expanding navy that ships' masters were prepared to take the risk of signing on any likely body. The ship eventually docked in Sydney, and Germy, having had enough of ship life to convince him that it was not for him, promptly deserted and headed inland. His entry was undoubtedly irregular, but I doubt if the authorities at that time worried very much about such trifles, provided the entree was 'white' and did nothing to attract the attention of the police.

Germy told me that while waiting in a queue at Kiel for his medical examination he noticed that the young man in front of him was crying. When Germy asked why, the youth replied that if he joined the navy he would eventually be killed, to which Germy replied, 'Vell, you vill only die vonce.' That reply became a family saying, as did his reply to the magistrate's question about his understanding of the obligations of a British citizen.

For several years, Father tried to persuade him to apply for naturalisation as a first step towards obtaining an old age pension. True to his independent spirit, Germy resisted the suggestion. At last he agreed and Father arranged for sponsors, and Germy appeared before the visiting magistrate. He did not grasp the meaning of it all and rather appeared to feel that he was on trial. I am sure that he distrusted the law in any shape or form, looking on it as an instrument which might hand him over to the German authorities. The magistrate was not getting anywhere and in exasperation demanded of Germy if he knew the meaning of the oath. Germy came to life and firmly declared that it meant 'kiss the Bible and fight for the British'. Naturalisation was granted.

The next move was to get him the pension, and that was even more difficult than naturalisation, but eventually Germy became a pensioner at the ruling rate of ten shillings per week. He promptly declared that he would keep five shillings per week for himself and that 'five shillings per week would go into the bank for little Alby (me)'. For the first time we learnt his name, which he gave as Fred Tivers . . .

We left Gooramadda shortly afterwards and never heard from him again. For all I know there may be a sum of money left by him with the NSW government in 'unclaimed monies'.

Before leaving Gooramadda, Father offered Germy a

home with us in Ballarat but he wisely declined. Father, I know, wrote to friends, and Glennon the policeman at Howlong, trying to find his whereabouts but nothing was known of him. Like the Arabs, he had simply picked up his tent and moved away.

It was a wrench to part from him, and, almost eighty years later, I can still see his nuggetty, shortish frame, kindly blue eyes and tobacco-stained whiskered old face. Looking back, I realise that he had a profound influence on my young life because of his integrity, independence and simple approach to life. Some of it stuck.

Well, Germy, whatever Valhalla you went to, may it treat you as kindly as you treated a little boy long ago.

CHAPTER 4

Early School Days

My schooling had been badly neglected. The nearest state school was two or three miles distant and, at age six, it was considered too far for me to walk. Distance has been devoured by the motor car and, in similar circumstances today, Mother would load the kids into the car and have them at school in ten minutes or less and would be waiting to pick them up in the afternoon. In 1904, Gooramadda had not seen a car and the only means of transport was by bike or horse. To drive us to school would entail catching the horse in the paddock, and those of you who have had any experience doing just that would know what a time-consuming job it can be. Like dogs who will go into hiding when you think of giving them a bath, horses have a sixth sense that tells them when they are about to be rounded up and put between shafts. Having caught a horse, it would have to be harnessed, backed between the shafts, and the traces attached to the bar; then there would be a half-hour drive to the school, so that by the time you reached there, an hour had gone by. The whole exercise would then have to be repeated in the afternoon.

At the beginning of the 1904 school year my sister Birdie, five years my senior and considered capable of making the daily journey on foot, had commenced at the Gooramadda State School, which was on the road to Chiltern. The teacher was a red-headed female martinet whose acquaintance I was to make the following year, when aged seven I was enrolled.

It was a beginning I never quite recovered from and I struggled all my school days. I had been taught to speak correctly by my mother and, according to my sister, that annoyed the teacher, who apparently resented it. There was one memorable occasion on which she, no doubt in exasperation because of some stupidity on my part, threw a stick of chalk at me, and my sister, eyes blazing, jumped to her feet and angrily shouted, 'Don't you throw chalk at my brother, Miss.' Dear Birdie, she was always my champion.

In the early years of the twentieth century, the area between Rutherglen and Gooramadda was mainly under vines. They were later destroyed by phylloxera and were out of production for many years, but have since been re-established. Our shortest route to the school lay through vineyards and we must have devoured many pounds' weight of grapes during a season. Apparently the owners did not mind as that weight only amounted to a 'drop in the bucket'. We were never warned off although we often passed them as they tended their vines and bid them good day.

At the end of the year it was decided that the daily trudge was too much for us, especially in winter. After much discussion and many doubts, we were enrolled for 1906 at the Howlong Catholic school about a mile away where the church substituted as a school room. It was an amazing decision as my parents were almost violently anti-Catholic. However, they had no need to worry as the gentle nuns never tried to influence our religious training.

It was a happy period in my life and I regretted it was only for a year. The walk to school was invariably full of interest, particularly when the river was in flood and the surrounding flat would be three or four feet under water, lapping the edge of the raised road. On every little island and in every tree would be rabbits, possums and often snakes; the rabbits in the forks just above the water, the snakes on the branches, and the possums wherever they could find a top fork away from a snake. There seemed to be a truce between the animals and snakes as I never saw a snake attack nor an animal display any fear. I, of course, do not know what took place after dark.

In addition to the bridge over the river and another long one over a lagoon at the foot of the steep hill leading into Howlong, there were a number of small bridges over the dry creek beds that became raging torrents at the onset of a flood, reducing to a placid blanket of water as they overflowed their banks and spread across the flats. No small boy could resist hanging over the railing of each successive bridge and watching the debris – mainly logs, trees, dead cows, sheep and rabbits – being carried along by the streams. There were floods every spring, and I remember one that extended on each side of the bridges as far as the eye could see.

Naturally Birdie and I would be late for school, but in those days when attending the Catholic school, it did not matter as we were excluded from religious instruction and prayers, which occupied the first half-hour after nine o'clock. In any case, the gentle nuns could never have scolded us for such a minor offence . . .

At the end of the year we were enrolled at the Howlong Public School, about a mile along the Albury road on the other side of Howlong. This added to our journey to and from school, but transport was at hand. Father had bought a largish blue pony (of course named Bluey) for the buggy, and family friends, the McKenzies, had asked Father to take, and thoroughly break in, a sprightly little pony they had acquired for their daughter, Jessie, who was about a year younger than me. Father was a very accomplished horseman . . .

By the beginning of the 1907 school year, the McKenzie pony was ready for me to ride and Bluey was spirited, but without vices. Many children rode to school. There was a paddock of perhaps an acre attached to the school master's residence in which we yarded our ponies and parked the buggies and carts.

The school was a one-roomed solid-brick building that

hadn't been altered when I passed it almost thirty years ago. It may have grown since, as I am told that Howlong has made some progress as an out-of-town venue for tired Albury businessmen. The headmaster – he had one junior girl teacher under him – was named Tweedy-Cocker to his pupils. He was looked upon in awe by his homespun pupils but was in fact a quiet and kindly man, as I discovered when I let his horse out of the yard. It came about as follows:

One day, opening the gate to bring my pony in, his horse had dashed out and run away. Terrified by the enormity of my offence, I mounted and chased after it. It headed for the common a little way down the road. In desperation I pursued the horse but I had no chance of heading it off. Around the common we went, Tweedy-Cocker's horse always fifty yards ahead. The common was riddled with rabbit burrows – it was before the introduction of myxomatosis and someone up above must have taken care of us, as neither horse nor pony put a foot in one of the burrows. Finally, with the pony in a lather, I gave up the chase and rode back to school where, in fear and trepidation, I reported the offence to the teacher. To my relief and astonishment, he patted me on the head and bade me not to mind as his horse had performed the same trick on him on several occasions. I was ever after his abject slave.

We were a motley crew at the Howlong school. Anyone who has read John O'Brien's poem 'The Old Bush School' can form a mental picture of the pupils. There were long thin ones and short fat ones and every grade between. The girls were fairly uniform in their dress, mostly drab colours beneath a white pinafore, and ribbons tied in a bow in their hair, thick navy-blue stockings and heavy bloomers of the same colour. Boots, black and mostly lace-ups, completed their dress, apart from hats which were of many shapes, sizes and materials.

The boys were in uniform only to the extent that they were all clothed. All were in short pants (mostly moleskins). Some were of knee-length, some shorter, but many half-mast. Shirts were almost exclusively blue and of a material called galatea, a hard, long-wearing material; these were, like the trousers, of varying length and mainly hanging down over heavy hobnail boots, always black and seldom licked with blacking. Those were the days before Nugget and Kiwi. The hats were always of felt and had obviously been hand-me-downs in the families, mainly from dads who had worn them in the paddocks and cowsheds for many years before handing them on. They were all heavily stained with years of sweat and many had holes in them and the brims were sloppy with age.

We were not a very inspiring lot at the Howlong Public School but there were a few better turned out and better spoken than the others. These were our particular friends, the Camerons, Kathie and Colin, from a superior property known as 'the White House', about half a mile down the road from the school. The friendship between Kathie and Birdie lasted during their lifetimes but I never saw Colin after leaving Gooramadda. I did hear, however, that he was farming somewhere in the Riverina. Then there was Gerry Hamilton, the son of the local storekeeper, but more about him later.

The time was 1907 and Australia was just emerging from its pioneering stage: it was only seventy-two years since the foundation of Melbourne and fifty-six after the establishment of Victoria as a state, and hygiene, especially in remote areas, was little cultivated. Consequently, many children had nits in their hair, and anyone seen scratching his or her head was douched mainly with kerosene.

Every morning before going into school we would line up in front of the flagpole in the school ground and the flag would be raised by the pupil awarded the honour because of good behaviour or good marks. We would stand to a fidgety attention during the flag raising, then salute it with great gusto, sing the first verse of 'God Save the King', recite a pledge with hand on heart to honour and obey the King (the Oath of Allegiance), and march to the beat of a kettle drum, our heads up and our eyes straight ahead to the school.

We genuinely believed that one British person could lick half a dozen foreigners. It took a catastrophic war to dispel that illusion.

The curriculum consisted of Writing, Reading, History and Geography. The starting point was the alphabet and multiplication tables, but I had already done these at other schools. They were essential subjects and the master and his cane would make sure we learnt them. Not that the master used his cane very much and the junior teacher, of whom, strangely, I have little recollection, administered corporal punishment only by rapping knuckles or the head with a ruler.

Religious instruction took place once a week and was delivered by a visiting Protestant clergyman.

The schoolroom was like an oven in the summer and an ice-chest in the winter, and chilblains were very prevalent. Practically every child had a bag of straw into which he put his feet, muddy boots included. This, plus some warmth from our open fireplace, helped keep us reasonably warm.

Like the ceiling of John O'Brien's 'The Old Bush School', that of the Howlong school was liberally littered with pens, some with their paper still attached to the end of them. Likewise, the pine desks all had numerous initials carved into them, it seemingly being a point of honour for each succeeding generation to leave its mark.

We were left to make our own sport, which consisted of marbles, tops, hopscotch, tip-the-cat, cricket and football and, the best of all, the odd paper chase. We mostly made our own tops, carving them with a pen knife from semi-dried wood or from tree roots. The game consisted of one boy spinning his top within a circle marked out on the ground and the others taking it in turns to throw their tops to try and hit the spinning one and either split it or knock it out of the ring. The first (if any) to succeed claimed the top he had hit if it was still intact, or received another top or some other article considered to be of equal value if it was split or broken . . .

Tip-the-cat may also need some explanation. A puck, of indeterminate length and thickness, pointed at both ends, was tapped at one end with a stick, which caused it to rise into the air where it was hit with all force possible. Whoever hit the puck furthest was the winner and claimed his opponent's puck.

We played cricket with kerosene tins or four-gallon drums for wickets and the ball invariably had many chips in it.

Football was played with newspaper rolled into a shape faintly resembling a football and wrapped around with string, except on those rare occasions when a boy received a genuine football at Christmas times and we were able to polish up our skills at the drop kick. Unfortunately, the ball would soon be punctured and the owner would withdraw it from circulation.

Best of all was the paper chase, and I have no doubt that it helped the development in many a country boy of those qualities of stamina and initiative which were put to good use by them during the Great War of 1914–18. The chase was generally run during the long lunch break or after school. One boy (the hare) was chosen by lot and carried his school bag full of paper torn into small pieces. He was given a start of a few minutes – varying according to the time in which we had to run – and had to leave a trail of paper behind him. He was allowed to choose his route. If he came to a shallow stream, he was allowed to wade up or down it, provided he left a clear trail to where he entered and left the stream. If he was caught, he was the subject of jeers; if he got home to the starting point without being caught, he was a hero for an hour.

The great event of the school year was the concert before the Christmas break-up. The highlight of the concert was the headmaster's contribution, invariably something from

Shakespeare. It left the audience spellbound. Cocker had a pleasant voice, which reverberated through the schoolroom as he proclaimed 'The quality of mercy to be still alive', but it was nothing to his rendering of Mark Antony's address over Caesar's body. Here he roared, snarled and swore whilst the audience were alternately terrified, alarmed and shocked. 'As good as Sir Henry Irving's rendition of Napoleon's soliloquy in *A Royal Divorce*,' proclaimed Mother, although how she could have known has always puzzled me. However, she repeated the soliloquy word for word. I was filled with wonder and pride at this disclosure of an unsuspected facet of a mother who had previously been known to me simply as 'Mother'.

I have never had a memory for rhyme or poetry yet I have never forgotten the following lines, although eighty years have passed:

> *Dearer than all in lifetime,*
> *Companion of my destiny,*
> *The only heart I ever loved,*
> *The only lips that ever stirred my swollen pulses*
> *My Josephine!*

Dear old Cocker, may his soul rest in peace . . .

There is little more to say about Howlong schooling. The education we received was sound and the fundamentals were ground into us. It was eminently suited to the times, in which there were very few secondary industries, certainly not in Howlong, and ninety-five per cent of the boys would go into primary production on their parents' properties or work as hired farm labourers, or on road work, or whatever rural occupations offered a living, however frugal. The girls would help at home – a few would actually work on the land – eventually marry country boys, in many cases those with whom they had gone to school, and, in due course, produce and bring up a brood of children and look after husband, children and home. There was little alternative. Some from well-to-do families would go on to a higher education and perhaps marry a doctor, a solicitor or a bank clerk, a shopkeeper or some such, but their fate would be the same, although probably in more comfortable circumstances. Not a bad fate really and, although downgraded in these modern times, Motherhood remains the noblest vocation open to any woman.

CHAPTER 5

Notables and Others

All congregations of people in cities or hamlets have their local notables and oddbods, and Howlong was no exception. A lot of them I would not have noticed or heard of. I was about five years old when we went to Gooramadda and eleven when we left, but some people I clearly remember . . .

The top in the colourful category was, undoubtedly, Mounted Constable Glennon, the only policeman between Albury, Corowa and Howlong. He had no jurisdiction in Victoria and there was argument in official circles as to where that ended. Victoria claimed it ended at an imaginary line down the centre of the Murray River whereas NSW claimed its boundaries to the water's edge at the Victorian bank. However Mounted Constable Glennon was understood to work on the assumption that anybody in the river was beyond apprehension by him.

He was an accomplished horseman and always spotlessly turned out. His lean, tall figure was built for the uniform and the saddle. The uniform was striking, consisting of skin-tight white corduroy trousers, black wellington boots polished to an eye-dazzling shine, a high-collared tight-fitting blue jacket with brass buttons and a blue peaked cap, more like the cap of the British Cavalry officer of the Boer War period than the caps worn by the police today. A riding whip and spurs completed his uniform. Like his boots, his saddle was glitteringly polished, his bridle and reins clean and supple, and the silver and metal of the bit, stirrups and spurs polished to perfection. He was greatly admired, especially by the youngsters, and I often heard mention of the conscientious manner in which he carried out his duties, particularly in the constant patrol of his large area.

It must have been galling to him that, no matter what the need, he could not lay a hand on a recreant a few yards away on the Victorian side of the river. This story did the rounds: a farmer from some twenty miles distant sent a boy in to advise Mr Glennon of the theft during the night of a valuable horse from his stable. Glennon had been trying to catch up with a notorious horse thief known to be operating in the district. He therefore set out and traced his man to a wayside pub some ten or twelve miles from where the horse had been stolen. The thief had arrived at the pub early that morning and, having been up all night, engaged a room and promptly fell asleep, leaving the horse to be stabled by the landlord. Glennon tied his horse to the hitching rail and entered the hotel just as the thief, apparently warned of his approach, slipped out of the back room, doubled around the building and, mounting the constable's horse, headed for the river and sanctuary. By the time Glennon had saddled the stolen horse, which like the thief was somewhat jaded, the horse thief was a good mile ahead in his dash to the river. Glennon arrived just as the thief, having abandoned his horse and swum the river, was leaving the water into Victoria – and safety.

Several years later, whilst attending a Ballarat Agricultural Show, my father spotted the thief, whom he recognised from the photo posters he had seen years before advertising a reward for his arrest. The thief was now the proprietor of a buckjumping show. We landed in a marquee in the showground and no sooner had we sat down than the buckjumping proprietor sat down directly opposite us on the other side of the table. He was waiting for his meal when Father leaned across the table and said 'Been around Howlong lately?' The man addressed looked very startled and declared that Father was mistaken as he had never been near Howlong and his name was not —. He was, however, obviously uneasy and left the table halfway through his meal. Father was at the show the following day and found the buckjumping show had disappeared . . .

The blacksmith, whose smithy we passed on our way to and from school, was like Tennyson's 'Mighty Man' – an object of veneration. We knew him quite well as he shod our ponies and horses and we had the run of his smithy – that is, Gerry Hamilton and I – provided we did not interfere with him, his striker or his tools. He was a kindly man and

I never remember him scolding so I assume we behaved ourselves. At that time, the blacksmith was the counterpart of
the garage and service station. He kept the legs running and
the wheels turning . . .

The Kelly bushranging gang were in the Howlong area
before the murder of three policemen at Wombat State
Forest on 26 October 1878, and there were reportedly sym-
pathisers in the district. As a boy, Father had lived close to
the Kellys outside Kilmore, and once he pointed out to me
an old, grey-bearded man who was supposed to have been
an active supporter. I believe the stigma still stuck and the
old man was invariably shunned by the locals. In his book
Recollections of a Victorian Police Officer, Inspecting Super-
intendent John Sadleri, who took a prominent role in the
search for and eventual destruction of the Kellys, records
that *'they were near Howlong on 31 October 1878 and that they
were stopped by the flooded state of the river and appeared at a
farmhouse, the owner of which was at the time under sentence
for horse stealing, in which the Kellys were associated with him.'*
The police arrived a few minutes too late and by the time
they reached the river, which had been crossed by the Kellys
despite the rapidly rising waters, it was no longer fordable.
Perhaps the horse thief was the old man referred to above.
The Kellys were on the Victorian (Gooramadda) side of the
river and must have been very close to where we lived.

CHAPTER 6

Family, Relatives, Pets and Fashions

My parents were honourable and good-living people, and loving and caring parents. They came from middle-class families and had the rigid moral outlook of the time. They took a great interest in church affairs and seldom missed a service. Corporal punishment was given only when well deserved, and never amounted to more than a slap from Mother. Father never laid a hand on me except for some long-forgotten misdemeanour, and only then because he failed to catch me. According to my sister Birdie, I had crawled through a hole in the back fence hardly wide enough to squeeze through, without shortening my stride, with Father, buggy whip in hand, hot on my heels. I know it took me several hours to summon up enough courage to go home, where to my great relief no mention was made of the incident, Father apparently believing that the fright I had received would be sufficient to deter me from repeating the wrong.

We always said grace before meals and prayers before bed. The latter practice was gradually dropped, but grace continued until my parents were forced by advancing years to give up their home and move in with Birdie.

Father took an active interest in our games and could outrun the combined team of Kyles – Birdie and me – and Rutzous despite a foot without a big toe – it having been blown off when, as a young man, he had rested the barrel of a twelve-bore shotgun on his feet whilst investigating some fault in it and it had fired. As a young man he was credited with having run a hundred yards in ten seconds.

Father was one of the best raconteurs I had ever heard and would keep us enthralled around the fire of a winter's night by tales of his early days in and around Echuca. He and Mother's brother, Alf Clark, had been inseparable and had hunted kangaroo, emus and wild pigs far and wide. Much of the country in the 1880s was still heavily timbered and game was plentiful, and killing it was not considered cruelty. Settlement was still in the pioneering stage and, while the big landowners normally had it very good, for the smallholder it was a constant struggle against drought, plagues of grasshoppers and the depredations of all grass- and flesh-eating animals including the myriads of rabbits. Hunting kangaroos and emus was not as one-sided as it sounds, for both (especially the roo) when cornered could rip a dog open with sharp and powerful claws, and if forced into water the roos often drowned the inexperienced dog by clasping its head in their front claws and forcing it beneath the surface.

They were exciting stories and I doubt if they lost anything in the telling. Perhaps Pope's very human couplet applies:

All who told it added something new,
and all who heard it made enlargements too.

One of Father's 'parlour tricks' was to imitate with bellows (a very necessary piece of equipment) the sounds of the engines of the various paddlesteamers as they approached Echuca, starting with a whisper and gradually working up to the best bellows could produce.

Mother ensured that we were always well fed and clothed. Money was scarce as Father, although on a reasonable salary for the times, insisted on paying the overdraft and other debts he had incurred during his few disastrous years in Corowa, although the bank manager and his other creditors had urged him to file his schedule – in other words, go bankrupt. They could have put him through the Bankruptcy Court but accepted his undertaking, and eventually they were all paid in full. In Father's book you simply paid your debts and he looked upon recourse to the law as dishonourable. Money, or the lack of it, was never discussed before the children and it was not until I had grown to manhood that Mother told me of the earlier struggle of our wonderful father and, to my thinking, our equally wonderful mother.

Mother made all my clothes except my Sunday best, which consisted of a navy-blue serge coat and trousers and white shirt with, of course, the customary black boots and navy-blue woollen socks. The coat and trousers were some sizes too big when bought, and sleeves and trousers had to be taken up several inches, and were lengthened as I grew until, in a few years, the suit fitted me. The tightening process then commenced until I acquired a new suit. The colour was always blue until, at the age of fifteen, I had my last suit before 'long-uns' and, joy of joy, it was brown.

Shirts were of flannel and singlets of flannelette, all sewn on a Singer pedal sewing machine. That machine worked overtime as most of the everyday clothes of my mother and sister, father's work-day shirts, as well as Len's shirts and trousers were also made on it: Len's during school holidays when he would be home from Geelong to be measured for the garments. Occasionally Mother may have had dresses made by the local Howlong dressmaker.

It was the day of the bustle – somewhat modified from its late Victorian days – high whale-bone stays (corsets) and leg-of-mutton sleeves; collars were high and stiff, and voluminous skirts touched the ground. Stays laced up at the back and it was Father's job to draw them as tight as possible when Mother expelled her breath. Girls' dresses were loose-fitting and looked comfortable enough but they were never shorter than three-quarter length, and underneath girls wore thick bloomers or, in summer, white (mainly calico) drawers, which were of knee length and normally finished off with stiff lace around the bottom of the legs.

Hats changed from season to season, varying from the undecorated straw-decker to small straw ones with flowers, progressing in size and decoration until, over several seasons, they reached a size, when, in the colloquial language of the day, they became known as 'cart wheelers'. At this stage, they resembled a small bed of heavily blooming flowers. Those who favoured birds started off with feathers and went up the scale until the hats were decorated with stuffed birds. Kid gloves and a veil would always be worn. To add the finishing touch, a fur and mitt would be worn in winter and, preferably, a feather boa in spring and autumn; the feather being usually ostrich with the boa hanging down to about knee level, or one end thrown back over a shoulder. The feathers were sometimes dyed. Most were imported from South Africa but some were grown, I think, in Victoria and certainly in South Australia.

The 'pill box' hat was very popular for a season or two. It was in appearance just like an enlarged round pill box. Hats were invariably bought in Melbourne as were dresses for 'best' as distinct from the everyday variety. This was the day of the cash-order stores of Fitzroy and Prahran such as Foy & Gibsons and McLennan's Big Store, which sent out mammoth catalogues. We children were always encouraged to join in any discussion and our views were always given serious consideration and we had great discussion, sometimes serious, sometimes humorous, around the fire for several nights as to whether Mother should buy a pill-box hat and, if so, which one displayed in the catalogue. This was the first year of the pill-box fashion and we all felt that Mother would 'lay them in the aisles' when she wore it at church. The one we chose cost the staggering price of one pound – quite a sum in 1905! Mother was a pretty woman and when she put it on with a veil she looked lovely, and I think that even Father was satisfied the money was well spent.

Ladies wore shores or boots, and girls almost always boots, and any girl who possessed a pair of button-ups was greatly envied.

Whilst Mother was the arbiter of our outsides, she was the supreme ruler of our insides. She was arbitrary in her determination to enforce a total cleansing once a week. Every Saturday morning, we (Birdie and I) were called into the kitchen and forced, under threat of reprisal, to swallow either a large spoonful of thick evil-smelling and evil-tasting castor oil or a cup of senna tea. They were both nauseating, the former being the worst. The castor oil of the day was greenish and thick, and more like grease than oil; the effect was terrific, as was the effect of the senna tea. On occasions, for a treat, we had Epsom salts, which was bad enough but nothing like the other two.

Saturday night was bath night; the bath consisting of a galvanised tin tub half full of water warmed by the boiling water from a converted kerosene tin and large iron kettle. We had to wash thoroughly and Birdie and I had to scrub each other's backs. The same procedure applied winter and summer, notwithstanding the fact that in warm weather we were in the river daily.

My sister Muriel (Birdie) was my constant champion and protector in my early days. She was a rangy girl and could run like a hare and, at the age of fourteen or fifteen, began to show signs of the lovely young woman she became. In addition to running, she could kick a football and throw a ball as well as or better than the average boy of her age. She married twice, firstly F. L. P. (Perce) Bawden, a fine young man killed in action at the battle of Passchendaele in Belgium on 4 October 1917, by whom she had one son, Stewart Kyle. Then she married T. E. (Elgin) Martin, an equally fine man by whom she had three daughters, Bessie (Mrs Frank Jelbart) of Ballarat, Joy (Mrs E. McClellan) of Pleasanton, California and Pat (Mrs John Ellis) of Ballarat.

The eldest of the family, Len, was seldom at home. He was living at the time with our Kyle grandparents in order to pursue his Geelong schooling. At the age of fifteen or sixteen, Len joined the Commercial Bank of Australia Ltd and died at Passchendaele on 12 October 1917, eight days after the death of his brother-in-law. Len's body was never found. I remember him with great affection. He was seven years my senior and was all that an elder brother could be. He was very industrious and kept himself in pocket money during the holidays by fishing and rabbit trapping. He would set numerous night lines and rabbit traps and would be up at daylight to collect the night's catch and have it ready for dispatch by coach to Chiltern, from where it would go by train to a Melbourne agent with whom he had made a contract. The fish had to be cleaned, placed between damp reeds out from the riverbank and wrapped in hessian, while the rabbits were skinned and gutted and packed in a similar manner to the fish. The coach passed our house at about

7.30 a.m. so he had a very busy few hours. The return was very small, about six to ninepence a pound for the fish. Those prices would be net.

And then in 1908 came Marjorie, who during her short life brought us all so much happiness. Born at Rutherglen on 13 March of that year, Marjorie was a lovely baby with eyes of vivid blue. They changed colour in later life but in every other respect her adulthood fulfilled the promise of her childhood. To know her was to love her and she inspired friendship wherever she went. She went to England in 1938 to further her studies in English Expression and Dramatic Art and taught at Forest School, Reepham, Norfolk, and Dartington Hall, South Devon. She had fallen in love with a Dutchman, Bernard Grasswinkle, the first officer of the ship *Almkirk* of the Holland Australia Line, which had taken her to England. She would probably have seen the Second World War out in England but for the Japanese threat to Australia. Feeling she had to be with her parents in a time of such crisis, she managed to get a berth on the *Melbourne Star* bound for Australia. She died at sea when the *Melbourne Star* was torpedoed by a German U-boat near Bermuda on 2 April 1943. Her fiance was later killed when his ship, of which he was by then in command, was sunk in the Mediterranean by German aerial action whilst in a convoy to Malta. Wars have not been kind to us, but they never are to anyone.

Whatever social graces we had were instilled into us by Mother. Father could exert a lot of charm, and was innately a well-mannered man, but there were times when he seemed to delight in acting otherwise. Mother, on the other hand, was always perfectly mannered. As the eldest of thirteen children, she had at an early age taken on responsibilities much greater than a child should have forced on her. She had, in effect, 'mothered' an ever-growing family to allow her mother to produce babies. Without exception, her brothers and sisters gave her a love and respect beyond that of most families to one of their number.

Living in an isolated and scattered community like Gooramadda, I had few playmates out of school hours and naturally turned to pets for company. In addition to my lambs, I had twelve or fifteen rabbits of various colours and combinations of colours. There were a few professional trappers in the area, some of whom had received kindnesses from Father or Mother, and, when it became known that I was interested in collecting the coloured variety, anything young of that nature which they caught other than in traps they would bring to me. I had rabbits of white, black, yellow, a very rare bluish and equally rare pinkish, and others in a mixture of colours. They made a rather beautiful picture and were much admired by visitors. Feeding them was a problem as fifteen rabbits can consume an enormous amount of food. Daily I would cut baskets of grass but the rabbits were never satisfied and we were forced to grow quantities of lettuce and carrots – a heart-breaking task with a rabbit warren fifty yards away. Water had to be carried in buckets from the lagoon a hundred yards away, a job that fell to Father who, naturally enough, became fed up. He made constant demands that the rabbits be turned loose, demands which were fully rejected. My despair was great when I woke one morning to find the hatch door open and the rabbits gone. Father was accused of letting them out, but denied it emphatically and, in time, I came to accept that I must have accidentally left the door ajar, but I retained my doubts. It was probably just as well it happened, as they had started to breed, and we would have had a problem on our hands.

We always had a dog. First there was a lovely and gentle collie named Jessie. She was quite useless around the place and made friends with every tramp who came in to beg tea, sugar and anything else available. We gave her to a couple of maiden ladies who killed her with kindness. The next was a savage brute named Ring because of a white ring around his neck, the rest of him being ginger. Somebody had wished him onto Father on the grounds that he was a good watchdog and a good heeler. Good watchdog he certainly was, so good in fact that no one was game to come near the place, the butcher, baker and grocer, who came from Howlong for orders and delivery, hello-ing some fifty or sixty yards away to ascertain if the dog was on the chain. He disappeared one night, and we never learnt of his fate.

Our next and final dog was a short-haired ginger Queensland heeler named Buller, and he was a gem. He was not a tall dog – about eighteen inches high – but he had a very powerful body and legs, and a large head with powerful jaws. He was not aggressive with other dogs but was dangerous if attacked. We could do anything with Buller and he never interfered with visitors or tradesmen, but he would not allow any of the passing swagmen, of whom there were many, to put a foot in the gate.

During the hot weather, when temperatures of 110 °F or 113 °F were not uncommon, we all slept out in the vine-clad verandah, half asphyxiated by the smoke from dry cow pats burning in an eighteen-gallon drum to combat the mosquitoes, which attacked in swarms. Buller slept at the top of two or three steps to the verandah. If Father heard an unusual noise anywhere around the house, he would quietly say, 'Go fetch them, Buller', and the dog would immediately set off on a tour of the enclosed house area, and then go to each bed and check with a gentle nudge of his nose that we were all there. When Marjorie was a baby, she spent most of the day in the pram on the verandah and Buller would spend hours beside the pram or with his paws on the side of it and his head between them while she pulled at his ears or poked at his eyes. This was not encouraged as it disarranged the fly net.

One hot evening, just outside Howlong, as Father and I were riding along the Corowa road returning from the Corowa Show, we caught up with a drover, his dog and a mob of about a hundred head of cattle. The cattle and the dog were on the point of exhaustion and hardly moving. The drover explained that he had to get the cattle to Howlong common, where there was water and he could hold them for the night and head for his destination, Albury, the following day. He was in a quandary, afraid he would not get as far as the common that night and, being a stranger to the district, didn't know where else he could find water without going through private property to the river. Father said he would get them moving and ordered Buller to take over. I had seen him 'heeling' a stray beast that sometimes broke through our fence from Costains, or, now and again our horse, but I had never seen him work a mob nor do I think he had ever worked one. Crouching with his stomach at ground level, Buller worked from side to side and back again, nipping each beast on the leg as he passed. That mob came to life very quickly and a quick nip now and again was enough to keep it moving at a good pace. Although it was getting dark, we saw the cattle to the common. The drover claimed he had never seen a dog to equal Buller and offered Father twenty pounds for him (a lot of money in 1906) but money could not buy him.

Before leaving Gooramadda for Ballarat, we had a long and earnest discussion as to what we were going to do with Buller. Finally we decided that it would be too cruel to imprison him in a small backyard and, after tearful farewells, we left him with Arthur McKenzie, with whom we knew he would have had a good home. After about twelve months Mr McKenzie wrote to tell us that Buller was dead. He had gone down to a paddock to catch his horse, which had been turned loose there, and had taken Buller with him. There was a strange horse in the paddock, drinking at the dam and Mr McKenzie told Buller to get him out. After Buller disappeared down the wall of the dam, the horse came out in a hurry, but Buller didn't. He was dead at the water's edge. It was thought that the horse had kicked him but as there was no sign of an injury Mr McKenzie concluded that he died of heart failure. Although very saddened, we were glad he had a quick and painless end. He deserved it.

Another favourite pet was Tom the cat, born under the house. Tom was the only survivor of a bush cat's litter and the mother went back to the bush. Father put the kitten under chloroform and desexed him, cut off all but about two inches of its tail and the tips of its ears. We never knew the reason for the removal of the tail and ear tips. Whatever the reason, it had no ill effects and Tom grew into a large and powerful hunter. He became known to the local rabbit trappers and, although they suspected that he sometimes gorged himself on a trapped rabbit, on the few occasions he was caught in a trap they let him loose to find his way home. One of the trappers who caught him told Father that the only way he could get close enough to release Tom was to prise the trap open with a forked stick. Tom would arrive home mewing piteously and with a paw three or four times its normal size. After a drink of milk and a feed, he would disappear under the house for a few days, after which he would reappear for short periods to be fed before returning to his hideaway. Somehow, the paw was never broken and after about seven or eight days it would be healed sufficiently to allow him to resume his nocturnal hunting expeditions.

Tom brought home many rabbits and possums and once a snake, of which he was very proud. One night he brought a fully grown live rabbit and released it – or it got away – in Mother and Father's bedroom. Bedlam broke loose, Mother screaming that they were about to be murdered and beseeching Father to save her, and Father frantically scrambling for matches which he could not find. While all this was going on, Tom was chasing the rabbit around the room, under the bed and over it, until the rabbit found the door opening and got away. On another occasion he deposited a rabbit at Birdie's feet. It was her birthday and, although just a coincidence, we liked to think otherwise.

An incident which I have never forgotten involves our friends, the Camerons, and it occurred just before we left Gooramadda for Ballarat. They had agreed to take Tom and, with Birdie driving, we took him over on the last Saturday before leaving. We had heard many stories of cats and dogs finding their way home over many miles. To guard against Tom doing this, we put him in a sack bag, securely tied it and placed it in the back of the buggy which, for some reason I never understood, was known as a piano type and had a tight-fitting cover over the boot. Perhaps the body was thought to bear some resemblance to a grand piano. It was about three miles to the Camerons and on the journey we crossed two major bridges – one over the river, one over a lagoon about eighty yards wide – and seven or eight small bridges over, at that time, dry creek beds. We released Tom on arrival and he immediately disappeared under the shearing shed, from where we failed to entice him. It was agreed that he would come out when hungry and would soon make himself at home. After spending the afternoon with the Camerons, we took a rather sad farewell, not only because we were leaving friends but mainly because we were parting with a much-loved pet. On arriving home about four hours after we had arrived at the Camerons, we were amazed to find that a plaintively mewing and very wet Tom had got there before us. It was a remarkable feat so, apart from the uncanny sixth sense which had led him home, he had swum the lagoon and the river despite the fact that, although cats swim well when forced to, they never voluntarily take to water. It would have been cruel to take him to a city so, very reluctantly, we took him back the next day and, this time, the Camerons kept him in an outbuilding for some days until he accepted them. They later wrote that, despite all their efforts, they failed to coax him to stay in the house for more than a minute or two at a time but that he was content, came for a meal when hungry, and was a great help in keeping the mouse population in check. He died some years later of old age . . .

CHAPTER 7

More Gooramadda Episodes

The next nearest river crossings to Gooramadda were Albury and Corowa, so it was to be expected that there would be a lot of traffic past our house, and so there was at certain times of the year, particularly early spring. Most of it, apart from the few locals, who mainly rode or drove, consisted of shearers and other station workers, carrying their swags and on their way to the shearing sheds of NSW properties. Many of them trod a path which they had followed for many years, from Queensland down the eastern area of NSW and Victoria – shearing at the same stations year after year – and some would go on to New Zealand and then back again to Queensland to start all over again . . .

The majority of these port travellers would call at the house if Buller (or Germy) were not on guard or call from the middle of the road if he was to ask for tea or sugar or meat or bread, some only for hot water. Whatever it was, it was never refused if Mother had it. She had spent her early life in what was then bush country around Mathoura and Tylden and where such requests were never refused. It was a 'carry on' from the early pioneering days when the country folk depended on each other much more than they do today. That spirit set the pattern for the mateship of our service men and women in later wars.

It must have been quite a strain on mother's resources as the requests were numerous, the record for one day being between twenty and thirty . . .

One of the drawbacks of Gooramadda was the lack of a doctor, the nearest one being at Rutherglen, thirteen miles away. When we needed a doctor and were considered fit enough to travel, we made the journey by buggy. On the few occasions it was thought to be unwise for the patient to make the journey, Father had to drive to Rutherglen to ask the doctor, or if he could not be found, to leave a message to that effect. It was, therefore, several hours before the doctor arrived, and his method of covering the miles was unique. The doctor's great friend, from a famous wine-making family, rode a motorbike which towed the doctor's pushbike using twenty feet of rope. It was a hazardous method of travel, particularly as the roads were full of potholes filled with dust. The motorbike was probably one of the first to appear on Australian roads – certainly the only one I ever saw during our years at Gooramadda.

Our association with the doctor abruptly ended after he lanced Len's neck to, he claimed, release pus, and found only sound flesh. This was done without any anaesthetic.

After this episode, we relied more than ever on Father's healing skill and on the much-prized book, *What to do till the doctor comes*. In our house, that book was second only to the Bible.

The great event during our years in Gooramadda was, undoubtedly, the building of a new bridge over the Murray. I am not sure of the year or years in which it was built but think probably 1907 to 1908. It was built alongside the old bridge and was, therefore, only seventy yards from our home. We consequently had a grandstand view of the construction process from beginning to end, and felt a proprietary interest in it. The bridge is still in use . . .

At last came the great day when the bridge was to be opened by the Premier of NSW, Sir William Lyne, in the presence of other high dignitaries. Sir William's position had an aura about it far superior to the positions of present-day premiers. Until the establishment of Federation the Premier of NSW had been the most senior Australian politician, and the aura of that position had not as yet faded. In rural NSW at least . . .

I was out of bed before dawn, collected Bluey from the paddock (he was easy to catch), scrawled a note to say that I had gone across the bridge and would be back as soon as possible. I rode Bluey at a slow walk in the dust along the edge of the road, and went so quietly that I felt that he was aware of the necessity for silence and was tip-toeing. There was no sign of life from the workmen's quarters as I undid and gently lowered the rope. I remounted, and the first step of the horse onto the bridge planking produced what sounded to my startled ears like a clap of thunder. No one who has ever walked a shod horse across the newly laid planks of a bridge on a still and frosty morning can imagine the thunderous noise it creates. As I dismounted to lower the rope and ribbon on the NSW side, figures showing signs of anger and yelling dire threats began emerging from their quarters. They were in various states of undress, some still pulling on pants as they headed for the bridge. Fortunately, the nearest little house was about one hundred yards from the bridge, which allowed me time, despite my panicky fingers, to get the knots of rope and ribbon untied, mount and head up the road to Howlong at a gallop.

I arrived home in safety to an anxious family, took my scolding, which I think was delivered with tongue in cheek, and savoured the delight of being the first to cross the new bridge.

CHAPTER 8

Huckleberry Finn

If I were Huckleberry Finn
What mischief I'd be in,
You'd find me out playing,
Beside a shady pool,
Wishing there never was a school.

This verse from an old-time song, which comes from where and when I do not know, describes very faithfully the pursuits of any adventurous youngster in Gooramadda and Howlong at the turn of the century. Everything – other than the blacks and the riverboats that Huck enjoyed – was there; the broad Murray a hundred yards wide – on which we had an old and leaky boat, swimming, fishing, rabbiting and pony riding from daylight to dark over the weekends and holidays and from four till dark on schooldays. Then there were the swagmen and shearers and casual bush workers, looking for, or travelling to, jobs. We moved freely amongst them and always received a cheery 'good day' or perhaps they would crack a joke with us or tell us a story. There may have been bad eggs amongst them, but if there were they were carefully watched by the great majority who were good fellows, and many of them would have had families of their own. Some of them may have been down on their luck and times were hard. The dole hadn't been invented and I am sure a great number would have been insulted had it been offered to them. The Australians of those days may have been raw, but ninety-nine per cent of them were honest, independent and ready and willing to give their best. They were also proud – perhaps over-proud – of their country and new-born flag. The education system had a good deal to do with it. It inbred in children a love of God, King and country, much of which disappeared with the First World War. That was probably all to the good, but it went too far, and a Second World War twenty years after the first completely changed the character of the Australian, not all but many. Probably the worst loss was of our independent spirit.

In the summer we spent more time in the river than out of it. Strangely enough, although I could stay afloat for long periods, I never became a good swimmer. Perhaps it was because of lack of competition. Occasionally we – the Rutzou boys and I – would race each other across the river and back. That practice came to a full stop when Mother found out about it. It was a wise decision as we were young and the river contained many snags, some of them dangerous with such decorations as trailing barbed wire, and there was no knowing where many of them were as they moved from day to day, particularly when the river was high. One example of this movement of snags could have resulted in even more serious injuries than Len sustained when he was home for Christmas holidays. He took a shallow dive off a steep section of the riverbank, at a spot where he had similarly dived the previous day, and hit a charred log a few inches under the water. The skin was torn off his chest and stomach and the whole area embedded with pieces of charcoal. After bathing and having the charcoal picked out with tweezers and his body bandaged, Len was ready for normal activities in a few days.

Poor Len, he had no luck. On another occasion he came home early one morning with a large fish-hook through the fleshy part between thumb and forefinger of his right hand. He had rebaited a night line on which he had a heavy sinker and, when swinging it around his head, he slipped on a muddy bank, overbalanced, and tried to throw the line, and the hook caught in his hand. Father had to file off the shaft and draw it out. After the usual dressing of lysol and a bandage, Len went back to his lines.

We had great sport drifting down the river trolling a spinner on which we caught many good fish. The pull back home in the heavy old boat was hard work, but who cared.

The river was not teeming with fish but it was a rare occasion on which we did not land several good cod or redfin. The most prized catch was a silver bream, a lovely fish which put up a good fight. Our angling equipment was primitive, consisting of a bamboo pole with a heavy cord line firmly tied to the thin end. A reel was unheard of but somehow we landed our catch; mainly cod, which, after the initial tug usually came up without a struggle. The silver bream and redfin were different propositions, but we landed the majority of those we hooked.

A great delicacy was the Murray cray, which we caught in traps made from wire netting. They were not plentiful but when we baited the traps we usually caught one or two. They would have averaged about nine or ten inches in length.

Yabbies were plentiful but I don't remember ever eating any. They were good bait and, whole, were used mainly for baiting night lines. The fish, lightly boiled, was good bait for angling.

During heavy floods, many of the dry creeks became fast-flowing streams, in one of which I came very close to drowning. It happened like this: it was a hot day and I was without a pony, plodding up the long stretch of road between the school and Howlong township with my friend Gerry Hamilton. He was three to four years my elder and the best at any game or sport, whether spinning tops, kicking a football, paper chasing, cock fighting or whatever. Gerry had sixpence and, passing the bakers', we were assailed with the smell of newly baked bread. Unable to resist the temptation, we went in and Gerry bought a steaming hot loaf. Mooching along, oblivious to everything but our treasure trove, from the centre of which we took turns in scooping out a handful and filling our stomachs with the hot doughy bread. We were almost in a sleep-walking state as we passed through the township, down the hill, over the lagoon bridge, until we reached a suitably fast-flowing creek. We stripped, and with a few powerful strokes Gerry was on the other side. I got about halfway over when the belly full of hot bread asserted itself. Suddenly, my limbs became leaden and I went under. I was incapable of making any move to save myself but, fortunately, Gerry was by my side in seconds and had me on dry land. After a short spell I was able to make my way home, a chastened and, I hope, wiser boy. Gerry, of course, was a bigger hero than ever in my eyes and even now, at the age of eighty-nine, I remember him with gratitude. He and I by mutual consent kept our mouths shut and this is the first time I have told the story. I doubt if Gerry would have told it as he was not the sort of boy to cast himself in an heroic mode . . .

Sometime in 1906 or 1907, Father took Birdie and me into Howlong to see our, and his, first moving-picture show, put on in the local hall by a travelling showman. It must have been one of the first of its kind in Australia. My only recollection of it is the terror with which I saw a team of bolting horses coming straight at the audience until they appeared to come out of the screen right on top of me. To my relief, the show ended there but the feeling of terror remained for some time.

The only trapper I saw on the river was in that period. First there were two journalists in a motor boat travelling from the source to the mouth of the river on behalf of the *Lone Hand*, a short-lived offspring of the Sydney *Bulletin*. I forget the journalists' names but I have a hazy recollection that one was called Brennan. I first heard the motor in the distance, beyond the bend around the Rutzous', and rushed inside to announce that Mr Morrisy's motorbike, presumably with Dr Kearney and his pushbike in tow, had gone into the river. Father, Mother and Birdie dashed out and we waited in fear and wonderment until the boat came into view. They stopped just beyond the bridge, and smoke soon announced that they had come ashore in our paddock. Shortly after, as dusk began to fall, Father and I went to where they had erected their tent, and Father, having discovered that they were without milk, despatched me to bring some down. Father invited them to spend the evening with us, which they did, and a very enjoyable evening was spent around a blazing fire. They had some interesting tales to tell and were fascinated by Father's stories of his early days at and about Echuca, so much so that I was told that in a book they published of their journey down the river, they wrote mainly in their journal of the hospitality of Mr Kyle and family and of his storytelling ability.

The next to sail past us was a man, his wife and small daughter essaying the same journey as the journalists, but they didn't make it. They were aboard a most unusual vessel, which was, to our inexperienced eyes, quite unsuitable for such a journey. It looked like a raft but was a shallow draught, broad-beamed boat, perhaps eight or nine feet long, on which was erected a platform overhanging the sides and ends by about two feet. On the platform was a small hut in which, presumably, they slept and took shelter from the sun. The contraption was steered by a paddle at the stern and floated down with the stream. They hit a snag and sank a few miles before Howlong but, fortunately, they all got ashore none the worse for their bath, but lost their floating home and their gear.

The lagoon at the back of our house was really a stagnant pool which was cleaned out and refilled whenever the river overflowed its banks. After a dry period, it became slimy and smelly, and the only creatures that thrived in it were myriads of leeches. Norman Ilsley delighted in standing in it and allowing the leeches to fasten onto his legs, knowing full well that the spectacle revolted me but that I would be forced to follow suit. It was useless trying to pull them off, but a piece of board on straight sticks rubbed them off easily. It was only about two to three feet at its deepest point so that we could sail or try to sail – anything from a bath tub to a discarded tank full of holes invariably with disastrous results.

In December 1908 Father was advised that he was to be transferred to Ballarat, mainly as a dairy inspector – the examination for which he had passed some months previously – and so the end of the carefree Gooramadda–Howlong days loomed ominously just ahead. Although the idea of living in a large city was exciting, some foreboding of the upheaval it would bring about in our lives must have forced itself into our conscience as we became more and more worried and, obviously, frightened as the day of departure approached. Even Buller the dog and Tom the cat seemed to be depressed, as though they had some foreboding that their world was about to fall in on them.

But dear old Germy was the most affected of all. I can still see the desolate old figure standing in the middle of the dusty road as Father, who was staying a few days longer to fix up the neglected odds and ends, drove us off in the dogcart to the Chiltern Railway Station to catch the Sydney–Melbourne train to as far as Euroa, where we stayed a day or two with the Palmers (Father's sister was Mrs Palmer) until Father caught up with us and we took the train to Melbourne and Ballarat.

The Gooramadda years had been wonderful years for me. I am sure Father enjoyed them and I think Mother and Birdie did but, by any standard, it was a lonely life for a young woman, and an adolescent girl. Looking back on it eighty years later, I am amazed at the living conditions compared to those enjoyed by even the less privileged today. There were no cars, telephones, gas or electricity, refrigeration, airconditioning, town water, radio, television, cinema, etc. etc. The nearest store was a mile away, but the store butcher and baker called for orders. The store also delivered, and you bought off the cart from the butcher and baker. Mother mostly made her own bread, and butter from thick clotted cream, until we acquired a small hand-operated separator which I detested as it usually fell to my lot to turn the handle for what seemed to be hours on end. Mother, with the help of Father, also made our own laundry soap.

And so it was goodbye to Gooramadda and a life of few privileges but great happiness.

CHAPTER 9

A New Beginning

After a few days in Euroa with the Palmers I had my first ride in a motor car. Uncle Albert Palmer had a car from the very early days of their introduction into Australia, and the present one, a Fiat, was a weird and wonderful contraption judged on modern-day standards. It was a vast affair; square with brass posts in each corner supporting a flat canopy with little lace curtains. Entrance was from the rear via steps, which were let down for entrance and exit. The passengers sat facing inwards on each side, and the driver sat in splendid isolation in the front. We were thrilled when Uncle Albert announced that we were doing twenty miles an hour. That, coupled with the fact that, according to some commercial travellers (one of whom had a stopwatch), our train had reached sixty miles per hour on our journey to Euroa, was considered to be an extraordinary experience and showed us what a wonderful age we lived in.

Weird as Uncle Albert's motor car was, it was nothing compared to his brother Arthur's motor buggy. It was simply a shapeless piano-box buggy with an engine. I am not sure where the engine was but I think in the boot; nor do I know the method of propulsion. The steering was by a rod, which was pushed forward and sideways (it would not reverse). I never saw it in action but was assured that it could do up to fifteen miles per hour. There must have been very few of these vehicles as I never saw another one and have never met anyone who remembers them.

After two or three days with the Palmers – there were four girls – Father arrived and the following day we caught a train to Melbourne en route to Ballarat.

Our home in Ballarat, 111 Frank Street, was a new house which had cost five hundred pounds to build and for which we paid 12s 6d per week rent. Our furniture had arrived but had been dumped anywhere a space was available. We managed to get the beds assembled so we had a reasonable night's rest. The house was lit by gas and the following night we were introduced to what to us was the last word in civilised living. Father had been down town and purchased some gas mantles, without which the gas lights would not function. It was necessary to put one of these fragile things over the gas jet, which was then turned on and a match applied to the mantle. The result was startling as the mantle was highly inflammable. After burning, it would disintegrate if breathed upon; nevertheless it was a great improvement on candles and hurricane lamps.

The next five years were uneventful but I found – and I am sure the others did also – the change from rustic surroundings and atmosphere of Gooramadda and the sophistication of Ballarat at that time somewhat difficult to accommodate to. Compared with the living standards of today, it was almost antediluvian. The lamp lighter came around on his bicycle and lit the street-corner gas light since electricity in homes powered by generators was a rarity. There was no sewerage, WCs were at the bottom of the yard and were emptied once a week, no matter what the weather. The milkman measured your milk into your galvanised billy can, and the butcher let down his cutting board at the rear of his cart and cut your order. The breadman placed enough bread to supply your needs into his open basket and brought it to your back door through hail, rain, snow or dust storm. All unhealthy practices, but we survived. Wonder of wonders, the ice-cream cart came round regularly and we waited impatiently, with our penny – or threepence if we were flush – clasped in our hands, for the sound of his bell. Domestic refrigeration was unknown and the arrival of the iceman to replenish our ice chest was a notable event and we invariably received a chip of ice to suck.

We soon discovered the Toffee King's shop in Sturt Street, on the south side, just east of Drummond Street. For threepence you received a large paper bag full of tooth-breaking toffee. It was wonderful and far superior to anything Howlong had to offer.

The use of the plural 'we' in some cases covers the two Ross boys and their sister, who lived a few doors away. There were others but they lived further away while the Rosses were my constant companions.

The trams were a constant wonder to a rustic. They were electric and very rattly, one-section affairs but considered by the locals to be far superior to Melbourne's cable trams. The power station from which they received their electricity fronted the lake about a hundred yards west of Pleasant Street and was a landmark known to everyone. School-children had to attend there, monthly, to purchase their concession tickets. It was before the day of Yallourn and each country town which boasted electricity generated its own power.

Wide and beautiful Sturt Street, with its gardens and seats and statues occupying the centreway, was a constant source of delight. The big night was on Saturday when the shops were open until nine p.m. and the City of Ballarat Band played in the rotunda in the middle of the street. The band-master and first cornet player was Percy Coad – proclaimed by the knowledgeable ones to be the best cornet player in the world – and we would stand around and look as wise as possible and comment knowingly on the band's rendition of 'Colonel Bogey', the 'Turkish Patrol' or Sousa's 'The Stars and Stripes Forever' etc, etc. Mention of the 'Besses of the Barn' would be sure to emerge and it was unanimously agreed that it was the world's best band.

These were simple, carefree days without any foreboding of the approaching disaster of the First World War. We were aware, of course, that the vainglorious creature, the German Kaiser, was showing his stupidity by entering into a battleship-building contest with England but no one worried about that. The British fleet was supreme and England was building two ships to every one the Germans built. Anyway, the upstart's uncle, our Edward VII, 'The Peacemaker', would take care of him. Europe was far away and there was no evident threat to us, although we were always dimly conscious of the 'Yellow Peril' but who cared about that? The British fleet would soon put a stop to any nonsense from that quarter.

In parliament, the Labour Party was an irritant, and a local fruit and vegetable shop owner had the audacity to stand for the Federal Parliament against H. V. McKay, the great harvester manufacturer, and beat him.

And so we drifted along to disaster, never dreaming that within a few years 70,000 of our best young men and women would be in foreign graves, many unmarked, or lost in many an ocean, and that the world would never be the same again.

Ballarat was a good place in which to spend those pre-war years. It was the largest city in Victoria outside Melbourne – population 40,000 against Geelong's 35,000 and Bendigo's 30,000. Its women were noted for their beauty and the men for their dressing and sporting ability, and the 'Golden City' was beautiful and vigorous.

The lake was the centre of much activity, with three rowing clubs and one yacht club. The paddlesteamers travelling between View Point and the gardens were greatly patronised on Sundays, where for sixpence for adults and threepence for children you would be uplifted by a pianist playing the

latest tunes, and often a singer – mainly tenors or sopranos – anxious to display his or her voice would give a
rousing rendition of whatever was being played.

For an extra threepence, you could go on a steamer taking you through 'Fairy Land', wending its way through the
groves of trees growing on the bank and in the water.

Having reached the gardens' landing, you were enter-
tained by a brass band performing in the rotunda close by
McIntyres tea shop, where you could buy ice-cream, sweets
and fruit and, if in funds, afternoon tea for ninepence a
head.

The young men, many in white trousers, striped blazers,
and boater hats that were fastened to their lapels by a cord to
pull the hat up when a gust of wind blew it off their heads,
strolled nonchalantly, cigarettes in mouth, about the grassy
area, ogling the girls in their colourful silks and cottons.

On the lake, in addition to scurrying steamers, there
would be a number of white-sailed yachts, each with its
complement of young men and girls in their colourful
dress, and hired boats, with young men anxious to display
their prowess with the oars to their female freight.

Then there was a visit to the gardens proper to view the
hothouses with their brilliant displays, and the statue pavil-
ion to admire, and talk learnedly of the statues there.

All very interesting and entertaining for a boy from
Gooramadda, if not on a particularly high intellectual scale.

Undoubtedly, the event of the year was the eisteddfod,
known everywhere as the South Street competitions.
Budding aspirants in practically every aspect of the arts as

applied to the vocal, visual, physical and musical aspects, assembled from many parts of Australia and sometimes from parts beyond, for the two weeks it took to complete the numerous events. It could be truly claimed that South Street catered to every taste from the very old to the very young. The streets would be alive with obvious vocalists, thespians, and children – mostly girls in all their chiffon – many with their chests encased in medals won in various contests. They would invariably be accompanied by obviously proud, deep-bosomed mamas also dressed in all their finery, many disporting many-hued necklets and clanging bracelets. Mainly they would be coming from or going to the Coliseum, a huge weatherboard structure claimed to seat up to 5000 people which was later burnt to the ground. Those not on the move would be practising their various skills and from hotels, boarding houses and rooms in private houses would emanate the sounds of warbling sopranos, deep contraltos, shrill tenors and beefy baritones going up and down the scales . . . If I remember rightly, they had up to thirty-two brass bands and seven bagpipe bands each year between 1909 and 1913.

The bands competed mainly on the Ballarat Oval, but many also used the Ballarat East Oval; all final events being on the former. There were competitions in all sections of band work including drill and marching, playing, and instrumental contests, and anyone winning the cornet contest, for instance, would be sure of a berth with any band in Australia. There were always bands marching up Sturt Street, and it was easy to find a compassionate bandsman who would allow you to carry his case and march through the oval gates by his sides. The gatekeepers must have been wide awake to that practice.

The most applauded winners were those who won the A-grade vocal sections for soprano, tenor, baritone and contralto, and it was a proud person who could claim to know such a one. We did on one occasion when a Murtoa friend of my brother Len won the prize as the top soprano of the competition. She had a lovely voice but used it only for the enjoyment of herself, her family and no doubt for charitable purposes. Many of the winners later achieved fame on the professional stage.

One incident I remember ended in near tragedy. It was in about 1912 that the committee engaged a stunt flier, an American, to fly his plane off the Ballarat Oval on the final day of the band contests. Flying was in its infancy and, so far as I know, no plane had ever been seen over Ballarat. The flier, known as Wizard Steve, entered into the contract without first viewing the site of the proposed operation. It must have been obvious to anyone that the oval, almost surrounded by high trees, was too small for a plane to take off from and the pilot, when he saw the area, declared to that effect. It was rumoured – probably incorrectly – that the committee held him to his contract. They had widely advertised the event and it was too late to retract. In any case he made the attempt, hit a tree, which turned the plane – a small monoplane – onto its back and onto numerous telegraph wires running along the southern side of the oval fronting Sturt Street. The wings were broken – and no doubt much more – and the pilot also badly injured. I had been watching events from a school friend's home adjoining the oval and we helped pull the pilot out from the plane. He was bleeding freely from his head, but was conscious and quite calm and later went on to fame as a pilot with the Eagle Squadron, comprising US volunteers, flying with the French forces long before the USA entered the war.

But to go back to the beginning of our life in Ballarat.

At the start of the 1909 school year I was enrolled at the Pleasant Street State School, almost on the shore of Lake Wendouree. I was eleven years of age and was classified accordingly to my age rather than to my ability. Consequently, I felt the disadvantage of my late start at school, but over the next three years managed to overcome the disability and 'go up' each year.

The years at Pleasant Street were uneventful. I made the football team and joined the cadets. It will sound strange to modern youth that a boy of thirteen could join a cadet troop, but these were the days of Empire, and Australia was over ninety-eight per cent British stock, due no doubt to our White Australia policy, of which we were also proud. We were, in fact, more British than the British.

The cadet uniform was a very colourful affair, being of light khaki with brass buttons, red stripes down the trouser legs, red facings on the jacket, with a puggareed hat turned up on the left side in true Australian fashion. In my case the uniform was enhanced by a bugler's badge – an elaborate circle of, I think, oak leaves surrounding a bugle all in gold.

I was a poor bugler and was forced to do my practice at the bottom of the yard, much to the annoyance of the adjoining family, whose objections put an end to any practice.

Towards the end of 1911 it was announced from the pulpit of St Andrew's Kirk – which we attended and where Father was an elder – that two scholarships to Ballarat College were to be awarded by means of competitive examination. I sat the exam, and although I did not come first or second, the examiner, for some reason which has always eluded me, put in a report that 'I showed great promise' and recommended that I should be granted a scholarship. The school council did not adopt the recommendation entirely but granted me a half scholarship, which was extended for a second year. Consequently, I commenced at Ballarat College at the beginning of 1912.

The college in those days was a plain two-storeyed brick building on the south-western corner of the St Andrew's church yard, and was transferred to a new building on the present site during 1912. Sporting facilities were nonexistent at the old site so we found the new site luxurious.

My two years at Ballarat College were mostly wasted. My whole interest was in sport, and I did just enough study to gain passes in terminal and end-of-year exams. In 1913, without any preparation or knowledge of the standard required by myself or masters, I stood for the entrance examination to Duntroon Military College, which had been established a year or two previously. The examination was held in a drill hall on the south side of the Yarra, a few hundred yards from Princes Bridge in Melbourne. Two hundred and forty sat for the eight vacancies allotted to Victoria. I did not gain a place.

I was successful in sport, winning the College Cup in 1912 by taking the final of the 100 and 220, 440 and coming second in the mile. In 1913, I was vice-captain of the football team. In that year, although generally favoured to win the cup again, I was second.

At the end of 1913 I applied for a position with the Bank of Australasia, was accepted and began work on 29 December. The commencing salary was forty pounds a year. I had to obtain a guarantee with a currency of three years for £3000 against defalcation: lightheartedly signed by a Dr Scott, a member of the college council; and my father had to sign an undertaking to, if necessary, supplement my salary to any amount required to allow me to live in the state considered acceptable to my position. The Bank of Australasia was English-owned and with all this, I was a supernumerary – i.e. not accepted as a permanent member of the staff – for three years. At the end of the first year my salary was increased to sixty pounds a year, at the end of the second to eighty, and at the end of the third year to one hundred pounds. Holidays were two weeks annually for the first ten years and three weeks thereafter. There was no tea money, overtime or holiday pay. At balance dates, twice yearly, we worked until two or three in the morning and, in country branches particularly, it was traditional for the manager's wife to provide a sit-down supper at around eleven. Some of the wives provided luxurious spreads such as roast turkey and cream-enriched trifle or such like, and the manager provided a glass of beer and usually a whisky for himself.

Most of the old-time managers took a fatherly interest in their junior staff and some would advise parents of their son's progress, particularly if behaviour and work were good. If the lad was a hopeless banking proposition, it was not unusual for the manager to drop a gentle hint to the parents that it would perhaps be wise if they looked around for a position to which he was better suited.

The social life of a bank clerk, particularly in country areas, was very good and he was in demand for dinner parties (always in the home) and for dances and other social events. He was usually a favourite with the local girls – and their parents – and the opposition was weak. It must be remembered that there was little, if any, industry – apart from shops – and the socially prominent of the town, as distinct from the farming fraternity, were the doctor, the solicitor (when there was one), the odd dentist, the bank manager and staff in descending order, some clergy and the leading merchant or merchants. There would be a few others such as law clerks, when there were any. Most of the youthful from these groups played reasonable games of tennis and football and golf – if the town had progressed to a course. They could dance and many sang a rousing ballad at the piano – some could even play – their manners were good, they dressed well and had clean hands. Practically all hotels, houses and some of the barbers' houses had a billiard table and many of the bank employees played reasonable to good games. Hotels were open from 8 a.m. to 11 p.m. except Sundays. I worked under a manager who was reputed to drink a bottle of Scotch a day but I never saw any sign of intoxication in manner or speech. He had one idiosyncrasy which caused amusement amongst those who knew him – his pockets were always stuffed with cloves, which he would chew after each drink in the naive belief that it would dispel the fumes from his breath. Perhaps it did but there was no doubt what the smell of cloves indicated.

Conditions in a bank were really Dickensian, and it took a war and a long, slow process of arbitration to bring about any marked improvement. Despite all the minuses, banking was looked upon by the middle classes as desirable employment, perhaps because it opened the doors of a slightly higher rating in society. After all, you can hardly be snooty with one who knows how much or how little you earn, and how much or how little you have in the bank.

After less than a month in the Ballarat office I was (at the age of sixteen) transferred to the small Western District town of Terang. The branch had a staff of three, the manager, teller and myself, a sort of dogsbody ledger-keeper, exchange and mail clerk. To do my ledger-keeping or passbooks I sat – as did the clerks in the days of Dickens – at a high desk, where the customer requiring his passbook or simply the balance of his account, could attract my attention by tapping with his hand on the top of the high partition separating the working area from the banking chamber.

My pay was increased to sixty pounds per annum by

the addition of a twenty pounds living-away-from-home allowance.

Salaries were paid on the tenth day of each month, when I received five golden sovereigns. My board at Mrs Shaw's establishment was one pound per week, consequently I paid her £4 6s 8d per month. I always had an account with the tobacconist – having quickly acquired the pernicious cigarette habit – of five or six shillings, which had to be paid if I was to continue to smoke. I therefore had between seven and eight shillings per month on which, apparently, I was supposed to clothe myself, pay my fees at the tennis club etc, etc. Of course I could not do it – it would have been beyond the capacity of Mandrake – and the bank very well knew it and, in effect, relied on my father to provide from his small means sufficient to enable me to present a passable front to its customers and the community in general.

Cigarettes were threepence a packet of ten, while Capstans and Three Castles were just twice that price. Those, with Turkish 'Abdullas', were about the only brands generally smoked. One other brand, 'My Darlings', tiny and gold-tipped, in a pretty box-like packet were produced for those of our girlfriends who were 'fast' enough to smoke, if only in private.

It was the day of commercial travellers and many large tailoring firms had their representatives on the road. These travellers had their own club and organisation in Melbourne which, in addition to providing club facilities, looked after their interests. In most towns, one hotel was nominated as the commercial travellers' hotel, and a notice to that effect was prominently displayed at the front entrance of the chosen pub. In response, the licensee was required to provide a large room where the traveller could display his wares on desks and tables.

The traveller (a jolly fellow) would call into the office and invite you to view his wares. Of course, being young and foolish, it was easy to walk into the trap. Having got you into his net and aroused your cupidity by lovingly display- ing all the latest suiting materials, ties, shirts, socks, etc., he would look pityingly at your shabby suit and suggest that he had just the right material at the right price to make you a suit that would be the envy of all who saw it on you. In response to your reply that you could not afford a new suit, he would offer extended terms – no account for three months, payment in six. Of course, I fell for it (Woods and Mason of Bourke Street were the tailors) and was measured on the spot and eventually received a beautiful Donegal tweed suit at the cost of five guineas. I was a splendid sight when I donned it and walked proudly to the office. My pride was short-lived as, before leaving the office at the end of the day, the manager (one of the kindest men I ever met) called me into his office and commented on my splendid suit and then asked me what it cost. On my telling him, he fixed me with a stern eye and asked if I considered him to be well dressed. On my reply in the affirmative, he said he had never in his life paid more than three guineas for a suit, and if he did his job he would report me for extravagance and have me dismissed as it was obvious to him that I would inevitably get into difficulty and finish up purloining the stamp money. I was never again happy in my suit. Of course, at the end of six months the firm wanted its money and I had to appeal to poor old dad for extra help.

At the end of my first year when my salary was increased, my landlady, who knew from long experience just how much bank clerks received and the dates on which the various banks gave their pay increases, promptly raised my board to twenty-five shillings per week, leaving me very little better off.

CHAPTER 10

War – 1914

O n 4 August 1914, war between Germany and England was declared and the British Foreign Secretary, Sir Edward Grey, prophetically announced that *'the lamps are going out all over Europe. We will not see them lit again in our lifetime'*. How true that proved to be. Australia's involvement was automatic, as a proclamation of war by Britain involved all her colonies, and a frenzy of patriotism took possession of the nation following the cablegram of Prime Minister Andrew Fisher to the British government that *'Australia is with you to the last man and the last shilling'*. Brave words!

War is essentially the art of compromise. In 1914, when Australia's young men flocked to the recruiting stations, the military were determined to send only the best to war. Five feet six inches was the required height, which at that time was taller than the minimum requirement for the British soldier, just five feet. Not only would the Australian fighting men tower over their British counterparts but the military authorities wanted them to be more imposing in every respect. The chest measurement was to be no less than thirty-four inches, bad teeth were rejected, eyesight needed to be perfect. Flat feet, corns and bunions meant you were out. It was a case where only the best would do, and in the recruitment of the 1st Division A.I.F. one in three volunteers were rejected.

Roy Kyle enlisted on 4 June 1915, by which time recruiting standards had dropped markedly and the height requirement was now the same as the British soldier. Moreover, chest measurement was considered of little importance so the wimps were included with the hunks. Corns and bunions went unremarked on, teeth and eyesight problems were largely ignored unless, in the latter case, you couldn't see the front site on your rifle. The recruiting age of nineteen was dropped to eighteen provided the recruit had written permission from his parents to join the army. Finally, the upper-age restriction of thirty-five was lifted by ten years, allowing veterans from the Boer War to become involved. Men were simply needed to replace the enormous number of dead, wounded and sick as a consequence of the fighting at Gallipoli.

In that first recruitment drive, when we were trying to put our best military foot forward, the general idea was to emulate the training the British army traditionally received. After all, this tried and proven method for whipping a raw recruit into shape had built a mighty empire and there seemed no reason to doubt its efficacy.

However, what hadn't been taken into consideration was the differing background and nature of the Australian, a colonial who had been brought up to think Jack was as good as his master. These were young men who were not accustomed to unquestioning obedience or to following orders, particularly when they thought them an insult to their intelligence.

The Australian recruit, unlike some of his British counterparts, had offered his services voluntarily and he believed this entitled him to a say in how he should be treated. He was hard put to see how poor rations, confinement to barracks, mindless drills and thirty-mile route marches in new boots that chaffed and pinched would help him kill Germans more effectively.

There must have been some anticipation of this attitude because over ninety-six per cent of the officers in the First Australian Division possessed previous military experience of some sort, most of them as militiamen. In other words, they had been part-time soldiers. Others had served in the British regular forces and a few came from Australia's own tiny standing army. They were given the task of whipping the raw recruits into some sort of shape by means of conventional drills, the application of spit and polish, and the inculcation of unquestioning discipline.

What hadn't been taken into account was that peacetime training in the militia hadn't gone in for much routine drill and NCOs were not overly concerned with putting a high-gloss finish to the appearance of troopers. Besides, discipline had never been seen as a priority for men playing war games in which they willingly collaborated. The Australian part-time soldier preferred field exercises, where skilled horsemanship, shooting and general skirmishing were the order of the day. This was a tradition adopted from the Boer War, where personal initiative was more highly prized in a soldier than square bashing, with the result that the officers initially involved in the A.I.F. possessed a poor grasp of routine military skills and were not overly concerned with appearance. Highly polished boots didn't make you a better horseman or help you to shoot straight.

In the prevailing culture there could be no blind allegiance to a set of stripes on a man's sleeve or two pips or more on his shoulder tabs. The attempt to impose what the recruits saw as unnecessary and unproductive strictures was to prove difficult to say the least.

The initial conditions imposed on new recruits didn't help the situation either. Volunteers were housed in open fields hastily established as camps without any of the normal amenities, running water, adequate toilets, shower blocks and canteens, or they were confined in city showgrounds. Uniforms were slow in coming, some units had hats they wore with their civilian clothes, others a shirt or a pair of breeches. Even boots were in short supply. The recruits neither looked nor felt like soldiers and, for the most part, wore their civilian clothes on parade. In truth, they were and stubbornly remained civilians who had volunteered to fight for their country and most had no desire to become soldiers of the kind that blindly obeyed orders or who could be made to meekly comply with patently pointless parade-ground discipline.

The authorities failed to see that volunteers would bring a different mindset to the business of soldiering. Most of the recruits saw the army away from the front as simply a new job and saw officers as their supervisors in a quasi-normal working environment. Those in authority were treated with the easy familiarity working men were accustomed to adopting with managers and employers and they resented the needless discipline imposed on them. These were young men who were accustomed to making decisions in their own right and didn't see how they would benefit if this prerogative was taken from them. They weren't conscripts, a state of affairs they equated with some sort of prisoner forced, against his will, to serve in the army by the government. Nor did they wish to emulate the British soldier, rather they expected to be treated as intelligent and sensible men.

For instance, they firmly believed that out of hours their time was their own and that restricting them to camp, where they slept on the ground under canvas or in a horse box or animal enclosure in the local showground was unreasonable when home and a comfortable bed was a tram ride away. They took to leaving camp and going home when the day was done, reporting for work again in the morning as they had always done. When they were dragged back like criminals, they deeply resented this treatment. While they learned, mostly by means of punishment, to distinguish the difference between army and civilian life, they refused to capitulate or to become submissive. Instead they became more cautious but no less questioning of military authority.

Although this form of Australian larrikinism was, in some sense, to be admired, it was not without its consequences.

When the 1st Division A.I.F. embarked for Europe just three months after Britain's declaration of war on Germany, they were still not fully equipped, and they were under-trained in basic military technique and unit manoeuvres. In retaining the right to be ruled by their own judgement, they had not received adequate preparation for the exigencies of war.

They would be fully kitted out and receive further training in Egypt, but by that time they had established independent standards of training and discipline that would prove difficult to alter. The Australian soldier, to the ongoing consternation of the British generals in charge of them, would continue throughout the war to be questioning and argumentative.

———◇———

Within a few months the 1st Division had arrived in Egypt to continue its training, and on 25 April 1915, they, with the New Zealand force, landed at Anzac Cove. Australia had felt the impact of war before – her troops had fought bravely in Sudan and South Africa – but never anything like this. Her previously untested men and boys had won a footing on Turkish soil against the best – a noted fighting nation could put against them. There was immense pride in the achievement, and confidence that Constantinople would be captured in a short period. Our ignorance of the position was immense and little thought was given to the cost because it was not known, and few, if any, envisaged the vastness and horror of it until the casualty lists began to appear in the papers a few days later. They grew from columns to sheets as the days passed, and the joy in victory subsided as the terrible cost became evident. The reaction was astounding and showed the calibre of the nation at that time. Instead of sinking into despair, the enlistment booths became clogged with volunteers clamouring to be inducted into the armed forces, and the 2nd Division was despatched a few months later.

After some long-range and strenuous harassing, I persuaded my parents not to oppose me enlisting. I know their consent was given very reluctantly and against their better judgement, but I was a well-grown and healthy boy, older than my years – or so it was thought – and they felt the need was great and worthy of any sacrifice; and God, King and Country was the order of the day.

Consequently, having put my age forward by two years and having been granted, on half-pay, leave for the duration of the war or until my death, by the bank, I enlisted and was sworn in on 4 June 1915 at the Sturt Street Drill Hall in South Melbourne. I was retained at the Drill Hall for three weeks, assisting the major in the swearing-in process of batches of volunteers. My job was to hand around the Bibles on which the Oath of Allegiance was sworn and to record the names of those sworn in a ledger kept for that purpose. This was not getting me anywhere in my burning desire to kill Germans or Turks and, at the end of two weeks,

I told the major that I wanted to get on with fighting the enemy. He told me to pick out a dozen of the men enlisting during the next week, and he would hold them until they numbered a dozen, which was the required number per tent, and he would then give me a letter to the camp commandant at Seymour, where we were to be trained, requesting that we be allocated to the same tent. In the main, I chose wisely.

The letter from the major, having been delivered to the camp commandant, Colonel Humphries (a second cousin), by the sergeant major, we were given a bell tent and shown where to erect it. This is where our trouble started. It was raining heavily, and continued to do so for three or four days, and the ground was a quagmire. Having erected the tent, we had to shovel out the black mud until we got a reasonably firm floor and dug a trench around the tent to keep it from flooding.

We were each given a palliasse, a ground sheet (waterproof), two blankets plus a greatcoat and, having been issued with a tin mug, mess tin, spoon, knife and fork, we were on our way.

Most tents bore a name in various colours of paint and, in some cases, tar. It was unanimously decided to name ours 'The Ritz' and I was deputised to purchase a small tin of red paint and carry out the 'signwriting'. I had completed the word 'The', when the evening picket marched down our line and were halted by a sharp word of command in front of our tent. The angry tone of the command presaged trouble ahead. Without further ado I was ordered to fall in and marched off to the guardhouse, where I spent a cold and miserable night and was paraded before the C.O., Colonel Humphries, in the morning. To the charge: 'Wilful damage to Government Property', the colonel asked how I pleaded and I stated I was ignorant that I had been committing an offence and pointed out that most of the other tents – and they were numerous – had names painted on them. This seemed an appropriate time to make known our relationship and I, somewhat hesitantly, announced that my mother, his cousin, had asked me to convey her regards to him. He asked who my mother was and I told him Lizzie Clark. He sat back in his chair, fixed me with a cold eye, and said, 'Well, well, poor Lizzie!' Five days C/B (confined to barracks), and that was the last I ever saw of him. Not a very propitious start to a military career, but prophetic.

The tent team were a mixed lot; all with secondary or tertiary education, and got on well together. Those I remember were Percy Brunton, a delicate-looking, gentle young man, son of a prominent NSW family, soon to leave us for officers' school. Then there was Archie Stodart and Claude Richard Guy Varley, the former in his early thirties, a large powerful man, a product of Melbourne Grammar, who left a lucrative law practice in Mansfield and fretted under military discipline, and the latter a dark-haired, brown-skinned man of about twenty-four or -five, also of Melbourne Grammar, who came from a family of printers whose factory was a well-known landmark on the south side of the Yarra just over Princes Bridge. With the exception of two others, whose names I have forgotten, both of whom were Victorian representatives at hockey, the rest have faded from memory.

Percy Brunton, I remember, arrived with a cabin trunk of beautifully monogrammed silk shirts, pyjamas and underwear. The trunk was promptly dumped outside and stripped during the night. I met Percy again on the concourse of Flinders Street Railway Station in early 1919. He was a staff captain and was a vision in gold and crimson. He asked me to meet him at the 'City Club' for lunch the following day. I spent a fruitless two hours waiting for him in the bar of the City Club Hotel, and as a result carried a sore head on the following day. Some days later I met him again and discovered I had been invited to lunch at the Melbourne Club, where he was staying. I never saw him again, and a few months later read a report in the *Argus* of his death at Panama on his way to England.

Claude Varley was different – an urbane, gentlemanly type, handsome as they come and fastidious in his habits. I met him again in camp at Weymouth, where I was waiting for a draft for a boat home. He was unaltered and the war seemed to have passed him by. He was on leave when I left for home and I never saw him again, although I read of him in the papers as a prominent land agent on the Queensland Gold Coast in the early days of the development. He once told me that he was the brother or son of a famous Australian actress of other days but did not enlarge.

Archie Stodart did not take kindly to military discipline. One evening I received a message from the guardhouse asking me to come and see him there. He explained to me through the barbed wire that he had approached the camp adjutant to request two days' leave to enable him to finalise urgent personal business in Melbourne and, on being refused, had told the adjutant what he thought of him in no uncertain way, which accounted for the guardhouse. He asked me to intercede with the little 'so and so' on his behalf. The adjutant, who was Captain Williams, one of our first airmen and later famous as Air Marshal Dickie Williams, head of the Australian Air Force, received me cautiously and, commenting that my hot-headed friend had probably learnt his lesson, released him after a night in the guardhouse and granted his request. As Archie left almost immediately for an officers' school, I know nothing of his subsequent career.

I found army life demoralising. The plunge from a life of reasonable privacy to one completely devoid of it was shattering. I, of course, accepted it eventually but was never happy being herded like a mob of cattle. Sanitary arrangements were, to say the least, primitive and the only way to keep reasonably clean was to trudge into Seymour and buy the use of a shower from one of the local pubs for a couple of shillings. The Seymour Picture Theatre was the only entertainment available. We lived, I suppose, just about as close to the earth as one could live, or so I thought at the time.

The tent crew soon began to break up as numbers moved into different branches of the army and after only four weeks training I found myself, on 16 July 1915, on board the S.S. *Demosthenes* of 10,000 tons, bound for Egypt, although we did not know for certain that that would be our destination.

The following day I developed flu and spent several days in hospital, missing the opportunity to see Fremantle and Perth. Our next call was Suez where we were entrained for

Heliopolis and I was allotted to the 24th Battalion, 6th Brigade of the 2nd Division A.I.F. I had first been recorded as being of the 6th reinforcement of the 8th Battalion then as of the 2nd reinforcement of the 21st Battalion, and finally was allotted to the 24th. The 2nd Division was being brought up to full strength to relieve the sadly depleted and exhausted 1st Division on Gallipoli. They were to be brought back to Egypt for rest and regrouping.

———◆———

Egypt proved to be an unfortunate environment for Australians. They were young men in search of adventure and they had no special interest in old tombs, no matter how imposing. They climbed the pyramids in order to scratch their names into the stones at their peaks, had their pictures taken mounted on the back of a camel and then looked around for something else to do. They wandered around the dusty museums, took in one or two mosques, taunted the apes at the zoo, attempted to get pissed on what the Egyptians had the temerity to pass for beer and visited the sleazy brothels in the Haret el Wasser, whereupon they finally made up their minds about the birthplace of the Pharoahs – it was the land of sin, sand, shit and syphilis and they thought even less of its native population.

Egypt was in every way a disappointment, after all, they had volunteered to fight the Hun, someone they thought of as a worthy opponent. Now they were stuck in a godforsaken land of shifting sand and wily wogs. They'd come to test their manhood and they'd not been taken seriously by Britain who, in giving them the Turk, had allocated a second-rate enemy in an insignificant location well away from the real action of the war.

The result was military anarchy. They took to missing parades. Absence without leave and drink and disorderly charges were routine. They gambled, fought and caused major disruptions in Cairo, commandeering trams by removing the conductor and making the driver return them to Mena camp. Charges of insubordination were so numerous that company commanders found them almost impossible to process. Assaults on the local population, theft, damage to property and general mayhem was the order of the day. They refused to salute British officers and would only take orders from their own and not always without an argument. When venereal disease reached unacceptable levels, the military authorities finally decided it was time to make or break this wayward and undisciplined mob who were masquerading as soldiers.

C. E. W. Bean, the official war historian for the A.I.F. wrote: *'Discipline in the A.I.F. must either be upheld or abandoned.'* He went on to say: *'Far from making civilians soldiers, the authorities feared training in Egypt was reducing recruits to rabble.'*

A completely new training procedure was introduced in January 1915 and on the third of February things finally came to a head when 131 intractable disciplinary cases and twenty-four men with venereal disease were told to pack their kitbags. The men with VD were sent to a special camp in Australia.

This action was partly effective on those who remained behind, particularly after a new ruling was introduced that there would be no pay for those with VD. However the military were taking no chances. All leave was cancelled and the new training regimen was conducted over extended hours, which involved digging trenches in soft sand, long desert marches and exhausting battle scenarios, known as skirmishing. The general idea was to exhaust the men so that they were too weary to play up. In addition, a formidable military police picket line was created across the Cairo–Mena camp road with instructions to deal severely with any attempts to leave camp. Some of the more difficult units were sent to defend the Suez Canal where it was thought the Turks might make a pre-emptive attack.

At best it proved to be a barely acceptable compromise. While discipline undoubtedly improved, due more to prudence and fatigue than conviction, the men's attitudes to those in command remained much the same. A.I.F. officers, aware of their men's attitude towards military life, knew that they had to earn their respect and often good-naturedly tolerated behaviour that would have been severely punished in the British army.

Bill Gammage, in his book *The Broken Years*, tells of an incident where a 2nd Battalion captain accompanying a brigadier on inspection noticed a guard on duty eating a pie. *'Hotly he ordered the soldier to present arms, whereupon the man asked the brigadier to hold his pie while he performed the ritual.'*

The Australians were itching to get to the fighting and throughout 1915 Egypt remained a troubled stay for the troops. The men were on a tight restraint, bored and weary from waiting, and eventually something had to give. On Good Friday, the straw that broke the camel's back came when it was reported that several soldiers had been stabbed in a Cairo brothel. Some of the Australians in the area set the brothel and half the street on fire, injuring civilians and preventing the Egyptian fire brigade from attending to the blaze. It was becoming imperative to find a scrap in which the lads could let off steam and it was fortunate that the Dardanelles Campaign was just about ready to get under way.

To sum up the entire shemozzle in the words of Company Sergeant Major G. S. Feist of the 52nd Battalion A.I.F. and again quoted from *The Broken Years*:

At Blackboy Hill I had to drill and generally make a fool of myself . . . When the instructor said left turn one would turn right sure as eggs, then he would condescend to tell you all about your relations, etc . . . when [he] . . . had taught us which end of the rifle the bullet come out . . . we were sent to Osbourne Rifle Range . . . Our section done some real good shooting so we only done the one course, worse luck – the shooting was the best part of it. However it come to a finish like everything else, and we marched back to camp about 32 miles . . . then we embarked . . . and of course we were put in Egypt. Days we hung about thinking we would have a scrap in the Suez, but it never came off. They dumped us off at . . . Mena Camp . . . it was rotten . . . sand, sand, sand in your tucker, in your ears, eyes, nose, everywhere, and anywhere, it was real crook we done marching, skirmishing and digging for weeks and weeks . . . I was heartily sick of it . . . we left . . . about 25th February . . . [and] stopped [on Lemnos] . . . eight weeks, going on shore, long marches and climbing hills, etc., getting fit; at last the word came – we were going to have a fly at the Turks. Well, you can bet it was like putting a bit of roast meat to a starving man – we sprung on it.

CHAPTER 11

Gallipoli

About seven or eight days after joining the battalion, we entrained for Alexandria at one a.m. on 29 August 1915 and there boarded the S.S. *Nile*, a grubby but fast boat which looked, and probably was, a sailer converted to steam. We had no escort and the skipper, who was reported to know the eastern Mediterranean like the back of his hand, took us on a three-day jaunt with the object of avoiding submarines. He was successful and we arrived safely into the magnificent harbour of Mudros on the isle of Lemnos on 2 September. We remained on board for two days, losing most of our money at cards to the Chinese crew, and on the evening of the fourth we transferred to the small steamer *Abbasia* and left the safety of Mudros for Gallipoli.

On 24 April 1915, the first contingent of the A.I.F. assembled on Lemnos, one of the outer Greek Islands situated just thirty miles from the Dardanelles. It is here where they would receive their final training before the commencement of the landing at Gallipoli.

The Gallipoli Campaign can be broken into four main phases, and although Roy Kyle was only involved in the final two phases, it is important that I write a little about the landing and the first four months when most of the heavy fighting on Gallipoli took place. It is within these two phases that Australia's first true military glory resides.

When I visited Gallipoli on Anzac Day, 1999, I was hugely impressed by the number of young Australians and New Zealanders who had travelled to the battleground to pay homage to their forefathers who died in battle. Nearly 5000 people attended that chilly pre-dawn service and it was undoubtedly one of the most poignant events of my life. It was then, as the sun rose to warm us over Anzac Cove, that I realised a new generation had come to embrace the legend of Gallipoli. I decided at that moment that, as a writer, I would do my best to ensure that future young Australians knew of the gallantry, bravery and sacrifice that had made this remote and inhospitable place so important to the history of both our nations. They needed to know, without necessarily resorting to more formal and overdetailed historical narratives, the grand legend that got under way on a small beach long before dawn on 25 April 1915.

The conviction amongst the troops as they left Egypt that the Turks were going to be a pushover was still strongly entrenched in their minds, they equated Johnny Turk with the Egyptians and, subsequently, wrote them off as just another bunch of wogs. They saw the Egyptians as a nation of thieving cowards up to no good who couldn't fight their way out of a wet paper bag and they couldn't see why the Turks would be any different.

It would have been a good idea at the time to have given them a historical perspective of the Turkish people. To point out perhaps that the Turks, better known in history as the Ottomans, created an empire that lasted just six years short of 400 years. For the greater part of those 400 years they controlled all of the Middle East from Iraq to Tripoli, they had captured Malta, besieged Vienna and controlled all the Balkans and south-eastern Europe as far as Budapest. Their navy, the combined Turkish–Egyptian fleet under Admiral Ibrahim Pasha, terrorised the Mediterranean until it was finally defeated at Navarino by the combined navies of the French, Russian and English under Vice-Admiral Codrington in 1827. But even after this, none of the great powers was keen to take on such a brave, fanatical and wily enemy on the land.

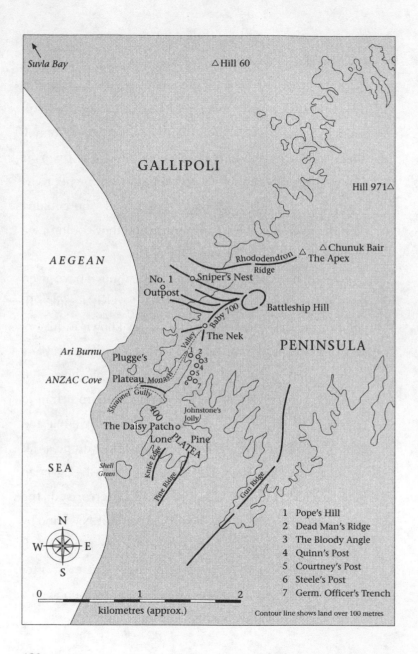

Suvla Bay

△Hill 60

GALLIPOLI

Hill 971△

AEGEAN

Rhododendron   △Chunuk Bair
Ridge   The Apex

No. 1   o Sniper's Nest
Outpost

Battleship Hill

Baby 700

The Nek

PENINSULA

Ari Burnu

Plugge's

ANZAC COVE

Plateau   Monash

Valley

1
2
3
4
5
6
7

Shrapnel Gully

400

Johnstone's
Jolly

The Daisy Patch o

Lone   Pine
PLATEA

Knife Edge

SEA   Shell
Green

Pine Ridge

Gun Ridge

N
W   E
S

1   Pope's Hill
2   Dead Man's Ridge
3   The Bloody Angle
4   Quinn's Post
5   Courtney's Post
6   Steele's Post
7   Germ. Officer's Trench

0   1   2

kilometres (approx.)   Contour line shows land over 100 metres

If they thought that the Turk may have dropped the ball since its days of empire they had only to be given a contemporary example of this clever enemy, one which had taken place only a few weeks prior to the proposed landing at Gallipoli. The first Lord of the Admiralty, Winston Churchill, had decided to have a go at busting through the Narrows and, if successful, would have opened his supply lines to Russia. The British and French ships began the bombardment of the Turkish shore batteries in an attempt to seize the Narrows, and the Turks, aware that they were potentially out-gunned, set up a number of large industrial pipes to emulate heavy artillery on the high ground above the fort defending the Narrows. As the battle commenced, the Turks regularly set off small amounts of gunpowder placed into the mouth of the pipes, making them appear to be big guns returning fire.

There is a further footnote to the landing at Gallipoli that seems to illustrate the careless attitude adopted by the British High Command who, as it turned out, may well have shared the common fighting man's misguided viewpoint of the Turkish capacity to fight.

Sir Ian Hamilton, the supreme commander of the Dardanelles Campaign, when approached by the surgeon-general prior to the landing at Gallipoli and told that he hadn't sufficient hospital ships and medical supplies to care for the anticipated wounded and, besides, had no way to get them off the beaches unless he used the ships' landing boats, is sharply rebuffed. Hamilton curtly dismisses him with the remark that the need to get stores and equipment ashore as quickly as possible takes priority over wounded men.

If the supreme commander had assumed a low casualty rate, he obviously had forgotten Europe's long and bloody history against the Turk. As it turned out, very little serious thought had gone into the evacuation of the wounded by the responsible staff officers at his H.Q.

In retrospect, Hamilton's rebuff and dismissal of the surgeon-general's needs can only be viewed in one of two possible ways. Either it denotes a complete lack of concern for the welfare of the men fighting under his command, or he shares a low opinion of the fighting capacity of the Sons of Allah.

If the first supposition is correct, Hamilton is not the only general in the war to have had a laissez faire attitude to the numbers of men killed and wounded under his command. If the second, which seems unlikely, for it was common knowledge among the officers that casualties could be as high as thirty per cent, then Hamilton is guilty of gross incompetence. A good commander, given the time, is charged with planning a correct outcome for both components, that is, landing his supplies and the evacuation of the wounded without having to sacrifice the one for the other.

Just after noon on 24 April 1915, the *Novian* carrying the 5th Battalion together with the Brigade H.Q. and the Indian Army Mule Artillery, sails from Mudros to the Bay of Purnea on the northeast of Lemnos island. Although they sail into a stiff breeze all the way, the weather seems to be clearing and by sunset the wind has practically died down. Facing the setting sun, the men on board can see five battleships in line astern, slowly heading for the Dardanelles and a place that will eventually become known as Gallipoli. On board are the 3rd Brigade, who will make the initial assault before the sun rises over Asia Minor.

The *Novian* slips its mooring and, under a bright moon, sails to the spot on the map where the Anzac landing will take place. It arrives just as the 3rd Brigade is being lowered into boats, each man carrying ninety pounds of kit and equipment on his back. Many of them must climb down the steep sides of the battleships using rope ladders that are swinging wildly from the weight of the frantically clutching soldiers ahead of them, most of whom are fortified with a liberal supply of rum. Even with the practice they've undergone at Lemnos, it proves a difficult and trying procedure, as it takes place in the inky darkness and is accomplished with the added strain of what lies ahead of them.

Fifteen thousand men are going into battle for the first time, in complete silence, jumping into little boats, which, to their great good fortune, are barely bobbing on a glass-calm sea. Above them the stars shine brilliantly and suggest a clear day to come. These are young men from a nation of beer drinkers, their heads a little fuzzy from the unaccustomed rum. Each wondering to himself if he'll prove good enough, courageous enough, praying silently that he won't let down his mates.

At three, the moon sinks below the horizon. The cliffs they could clearly see by moonlight now disappear in the pre-dawn darkness. The night is so densely dark that they can almost feel it enclosing about them. Only the soft pulse of the battleship's engines sends a slightly hollow sound against the hull to remind them that they are not alone in this curious and strange space.

It is an alien experience to feel so entirely alone while surrounded by your invisible mates. You have become accustomed to being identified by your group, your platoon, company, brigade, but most of all by your mates. Those blokes with whom you have trained, who crawled sweating beside you in the sand under a blazing desert sun, to whom you clung, bunched together on the platform of a tram to Cairo, with whom you got drunk on arak in the bazaar, laughed with and backslapped each other, chundered in an alley while your mates steadied you, jeered, chaffed and constantly mocked one another. All of these things have been with you for the past few months, you know your mates by the sounds they make, the pitch of their voices, the nature of their wisecracks, their stupidity, shrewdness, shyness, boastfulness, bullshitting, modesty and easygoing comradeship. You can't imagine yourself as a separate part of the whole, or them no longer a part of your life. And now, when you are about to face the moment of truth, they are silent, you are silent, all the familiar touchstones have disappeared in the inky darkness. In the pre-dawn chill there is only the creak of the rowlocks and the slap of a small, calm wave against the hull of the wooden lifeboat. Now you belong to your own silence, this is your true identity as you prepare to go into battle.

You are aware for the first time since you stood in the recruitment queue that you are alone, a single unit, the hard flat wooden seat under your arse turning it numb, and the heavy pack on your back the only extension of yourself you are aware of. One towel, one extra vest, socks, two pairs, greatcoat, cap, comforter, a change of underclothing (must die with clean underpants), three empty sandbags rolled and neatly tied onto your entrenching tool. Three days of rations – two tins of bullybeef, Fray Bentos (doesn't sound Australian), three pounds of hard biscuits (the ones Arnott's had left over from the Boer War). Then the little white bag of iron rations tied around your neck, half an ounce of tea (no fuckin' billy), two ounces of sugar and a jar of extract of beef. Two hundred rounds of ammunition, your rifle and bayonet, the killing load three times as heavy as the food that is meant to sustain you for the next seventy-two hours, that is, if you're not shot right off, coming out of the shallows with this burden on your shoulders forcing you downwards so that you drown in a mixture of salt water and blood.

In the moonlight you clearly see the cliffs and the land rising steeply up from the sea, and then further to the north the flat land where you expect they'll put you ashore. Now you face only darkness. A darkness where men like you, with cold hands and broken fingernails, blow on their clenched fists and wait on the cliffs and trenches, their rifles and machine guns oiled like your own, barrels cleaned, with spare charger clips and ammunition belts in reserve. They are waiting for you to arrive, to set foot onto the soil of their beloved country.

They wait on the same hills, facing the same coastline where their ancestors fought the Greeks and the Romans, and where they repulsed the Infidel Crusaders carrying their tortured Holy Cross before them into battle, their emaciated bodies and fair skins burnt a crimson colour and their hard, hollow eyes fixed on the cross, prepared to die in the name of the Prophet Christ. Then there were the strutting cocks, the French, and the pompous, over-confident British lions, both braided in gold and uniformed in red and blue, both nations vainglorious and arrogant to the point of infinite stupidity, and once again they are clawing at your neck. And, as always, the bearded Russian bear is trying to shoulder his way through your narrow and fanatically guarded sea lanes, determined to sever the very arteries of your existence. The bear is a slow learner and you keep singeing his fur and sending him scurrying back into the safety of his landlocked sea until his next memory loss.

And now, with spring arrived and the hope of new wheat already turning the ploughed land green, the tender shoots broken through the winter-hardened clods and the first of the scarlet poppies in bloom on the thistle- and weed-fringed edges of the fields, comes a new tribe of men. Giants with loose shoulders and gangling easygoing strides, infidels who have come from somewhere near the bottom of the world and who are determined to destroy you, murder your children and rape your wives.

And so once again the Turks must take up arms and, in the name of the Prophet, must show the enemy their sharp, snarling teeth and be prepared to repel the invader and to die fearlessly in the name of Allah and so gain a place in Paradise.

The landing boats are in four long lines with a little coal-fired pinnacle, its stack billowing smoke into the dark night, responsible for towing each line to within a hundred yards of the shore. It is slow work and with the exception of the soft throb of the steam engines on the sturdy little boats, one has to marvel at the quiet. How can so many young men remain so still when they know that one in three of them will be dead or wounded before the sun sets?

Suddenly the smokestack of one of the pinnacles sets on fire, the flames leaping high, exaggerated in the surrounding darkness, sending a signal for miles, the mirror-calm sea kicking back the reflection of the flames across a wide bay. Yet there is no response from the cliffs lining the shore, which, as they draw ever closer, begin to loom up, dark unwelcoming fortresses where the enemy waits. The silence, the unending silence, remains.

Then there is a shout, sudden and clear across the

water. 'You are going the wrong way, bear over.' The voice is like a sudden obscenity breaking into the silence. It calls again. 'Bear right, bear to starboard!' But to no avail, the pinnacle doesn't change course, it is as if its rudder is stuck. What does the suddenly shouted instruction mean? How far are you off course? In the dark how does the voice know anyway? You can't see him so how can he see you? Why doesn't the pinnacle bear to starboard, that's where in the moonlight you observed the flat ground, wasn't it? Any idjit can steer a flamin' boat when the water is still as a mill pond.

And then the pinnacle cuts the rowboats loose and the rowers take over, moving slowly into the beach, the men behind the oars grunting and sweating in the dawn cold, their oars splashing as the waves created by the prows of the landing boats ahead are beginning to build up.

There is a sudden sharp flash of a searchlight in the distance, then another in the direction of Cape Helles. Neither reaches your own dark space. And at last a half-heard instruction. 'Righto, lads, over the side. Good luck.' You leap and there is an obscenely loud splash that follows as you hit the water, then relief as your boots touch the bottom. Tiny waves lap around your waist, your rifle is held in both hands above your shoulders. Still dark, still safe from the sniper waiting on the dark cliff ahead, although the sky is beginning to lighten. Then a single shot from the dark cliff ahead, its echo filling the silence so totally that it seems to resonate against the wall of stillness you've built around yourself these last hours. And, in the words of Lance Corporal Mitchell of the 10th Battalion, *'The key is turned in the lock of the lid of hell.'*

Several of the landing boats are sprayed by machinegun fire, killing most of the men on board, the young bright-eyed soldiers of Australia, alive one moment, preparing to jump into the fray, and dead the next. One soldier remains seated as his comrades leap over the side, his sergeant, last but himself to jump, sees what he thinks is panic in his eyes, the terror of the moment freezing him to the thwart. He reaches out to touch him, their eyes meet momentarily, 'There's a good lad, come now.' The soldier topples forward into the bottom of the boat. He was dead all along, killed without a whimper, the bullet not even disturbing him in his seat. And the bullets and the shrapnel fall like summer rain.

The troops thresh in the water, trying to force their legs to move faster, mouths half open, fighting a silent panic, trying to keep their heads. Some attempt to fix their bayonets. There isn't any point in firing a shot at the blank, dark wall ahead. Strict orders. 'No rifle here is to be employed before broad daylight, you have to see the enemy before you can hit him. Only the bayonet is to be fixed.'

Some stumble against a submerged rock and fall face-first into the surf, the kit on their back slamming them down like a fist to the back of the head, their arms and legs starting to pump adrenaline to get them up again. Others hit sudden unexpected depths and, flailing desperately, they are sucked down by the weight of their packs. Mere arms lack the power to save them as they suck salt water into their lungs; they drown wearing full kit in a circle of tiny bubbles. Others drop to their knees in the water with a soft exclamation, a low curse or a surprised bellow as a Mauser bullet smashes into them. They don't see the hole, the size of a baby's tightly clamped fist, or feel the churning together of lung and windpipe and bits of smashed bone as the bullet, made in Germany, enters their chest.

The enemy has their range right from the start and, even without being able to see clearly, fires into the dark wet mass milling together on the narrow strip of beach below. This isn't prideful work for a sniper, this is shooting fish in a barrel, firing almost without the need to aim. When dawn finally comes, the surf washing onto the pebbled beach is pink, turning to an ever-deepening crimson.

The order given as they board the landing craft is for

every man to fall in and fix bayonets when they arrive on the beach. It goes further even than this. Each man is to grab hold of the bloke next to him and hold onto his sleeve. In truth, if anyone had been stupid enough to obey this command, it would have been the equivalent of deliberately lining up in front of a firing squad. 'There you go, Johnny Turk, take your time, mate, aim true. We'll die brave men, steady and dead stupid, to the last.'

Instead, many of the troops have tossed off their packs as they reach the beach, some of them were smart enough to have done so while still in the water. Men of every company are shouting like demons, releasing the tension, making for the cliffs and any overhang they can find. Every battalion is hopelessly mixed, sergeants and officers scattered, yelling inanely for their blokes, just as panicked as the rest. Nobody is listening, it's every bloke for himself, and the terror of what's happening makes them helpless with their own fear.

A Turkish battery, concealed in the half-light from the guns of the battleships that have now commenced to pound the cliffs, bursts shrapnel over the cowering and panicked troops, fireworks from hell, a shower of hot bright death. Ears are not tuned to commands in such a state, orders have no significance, no meaning, it's all gibberish, open mouths shouting silently against the guns and no single command makes any sense.

Those on the outer extremity of the beach where there is no possible shelter from enemy fire will lie in the wash and the sun for two days before they are removed by night. Others, drowned by the weight of their ninety-pound packs, will float to the surface in the next few days. The boats and rafts bringing in supplies will become accustomed to the soft thud of a body as they bump it aside, for if there is no time to attend to the wounded, there is no space left in their minds for the waterlogged dead.

And so as the terrible light grows stronger, the Anzacs climb for their lives. The beach behind them can barely be seen for the bodies and the discarded packs of panicked men. Hanging around for orders means certain death, it's a matter of climb or die, clutching bush or thorn, root and rock.

Boots scuff the hard red soil, sending pebbles avalanching onto the beach below. One thought in every soldier's mind is to get off the beach, find cover, move upward, hope you see the bastard in his cosy nest before he sees you. Stuff the bayonet and the order not to fire in the half-light, slip a clip into your rifle, ram one into the breech, you're going to be too puffed to stick the bugger in but not to shoot the bastard. Slowly you grab a hold of your panicked senses, the beach is maybe 400 yards long but no wider than your mum's backyard and there's 15,000 men, or what's left of them, packed on it like newborn chicks in a hatchery. Climb, you bastard, don't look back, if you're going to die, try to get at least one of them first.

The immediate slopes ahead of them are very abrupt, rising higher to the north like the walls of some weather-torn and crumpling Crusader castle, gaunt canyons are set back slightly further from the beach and appear to be unclimbable. Once up on the slopes, the soldiers realise that they are in an even worse climbing predicament than they may have at first supposed, as the topography isn't simply a steep climb but is broken by deep ridges, curving narrow valleys and eroding soil forming crumbling red gullies twisting in and out of almost inaccessible funnels. Gravel outcrops are a perfect protection for the enemy while deep basins form perfect traps for the invader. The cliffs are covered with dense scrub, most of it consisting of a variety of vicious thorns. It is a virtual paradise for the snipers who, having had time to study the more likely routes to the top, can position themselves to advantage. It is not the height of the various ridges but the steepness, the abrupt changes of direction and the general slope that make it almost impossible for advancing infantry and virtually inaccessible for practical or co-ordinated artillery fire.

The entire battle area from extreme north to its southern-most point is a mile and a half in length and exactly a thousand yards (about 900 metres) to its furthest point upwards. In all, it is an area no larger than three-quarters of a square mile (almost two square kilometres). Unbeknownst to the frantically climbing troops, they vastly outnumber the Turks in position on the high ground and often enough rush past snipers who are concealed in this extremely sniper-friendly landscape behind natural camouflage and for whom there is simply too much to shoot at.

The sun is well up by seven-thirty when the second wave, the 2nd Battalion, comes in to run what has now become an even more deadly and well-co-ordinated gauntlet of Turkish shrapnel, sniper and machine-gun fire. The beach is now better organised, though, and once on it the Australians are moved relatively quickly into the safest areas.

The situation by the time the 2nd Brigade arrives is perilous. Earlier, the men of the 3rd Brigade who have survived the landing made no attempt to find their companies, instead, in the total confusion they've set out in isolated groups, 'penny packets', to make their escape and, when they feel sufficiently far away from the mayhem on the beach and come to their senses, they go after the enemy. Soon enough, some of the most intrepid of these unattached groups reach the first ridge. With the sun in their faces, their shapes are clearly silhouetted against the skyline. Those following behind mistake them for the enemy and fire. Suddenly those in the most advanced positions find themselves sandwiched between Turkish sniper fire higher up on the second ridge and their own rifle fire coming up from below. Many of them perish in a hail of misdirected bullets from their mates.

However, instead of taking cover and waiting for their own troops to catch up with them, they are driven forward by the sight of small groups of the enemy vanishing into the dark tangle of gullies ahead of them. As the Turks' shooting is dying away, they think they've got the Turk on the run and the time has come to avenge their comrades lying dead on the beach below them. They thrust further and further inland, isolating themselves completely from any organised attrition, Johnny Turk drawing them away from their own forces. They are further encouraged when some of the Turks, caught by surprise and observing the Australians catching up, throw down their weapons and surrender. There is no thought of taking prisoners, too many of their mates are lying dead in the morning sun and this is payback time, they shoot the surrendered Turks on the spot and continue in hot pursuit of the others.

The advancing Australians are unaware that the Turks had considered the possibility of a landing north of the Gaba Tepe highly unlikely, as it would patently amount to suicide. Not even the British could be that stupid, so they only have one company guarding the slopes, more as lookouts than as troops fully prepared and dug in for combat. Even in scattered disorganised groups, the Australians vastly outnumber them, though not far behind Sari Bair, the very topmost ridge and the most important objective for the Australians, there are several companies of Turkish reinforcements no more than half an hour's marching time away.

Shortly after nine, the first of the enemy reinforcements begin to arrive. The Anzacs are nearing the top of the second ridge, known as 400 Plateau, which is an important first objective as it is a prime location from which the Turks can best observe the beach to shell the Anzacs. Now seeing the enemy reinforcements advancing towards them, they realise they have been caught between the proverbial rock and a hard place as the Turkish counter attack has moved up the valleys, outflanking the Australian outposts on the left of the plateau, and the disparate and scattered invaders are driven back predominantly on this left flank where the fighting is fiercest. Other troops coming up from the centre and the right of the plateau rush forward to help their mates on the left, leaving the centre and right, or southern flank, exposed. In the ensuing battle a great many men of the

3rd Brigade are killed and wounded. The Australians are beginning to revise their opinion of the sons of Allah as they attempt to consolidate and regroup into larger, more organised groups and start to dig in directly under the lip of 400 Plateau.

By now the 2nd Brigade, the second wave of Anzacs, have landed. This time, despite the fierce hail of artillery, shrapnel, machine-gun and rifle fire, which is considerably heavier than the reception given the 3rd Brigade in the first wave, the troops are directed to an assembly point that proves relatively safe from enemy fire. There is still a great deal of panic on the narrow beach and the act of assembling is by no means calm and orderly. Officers and N.C.O.s often scream contradictory commands at confused and frightened troops, but somehow they manage to get a sufficiently concerted fighting force together. This allows the Australian brigade commander, Colonel M'Cay, to put together a force to reinforce the scattered remnants of the 9th Battalion, who are now being counter-attacked by the Turkish reinforcements and are grimly holding their positions on the southern flank.

M'Cay's orders are to advance across 400 Plateau with bayonets fixed to get in among the Turks on the third ridge. With no telephone wires yet laid, M'Cay is unaware that the remainder of the line to the centre and north is

Roy Kyle pictured with his parents and siblings, around 1914. Back row (from left): Leonard, Muriel ('Birdie'), Roy. Front row (from left): Albert, Marjorie, Elizabeth.

Roy (right) and his brother Len in London, 1917.

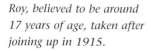

Roy, believed to be around 17 years of age, taken after joining up in 1915.

Volunteers queuing to enlist outside the Melbourne Town Hall, 1916.

Troops line up at Station Pier, Melbourne, prior to leaving on troopship A40 HMT Ceramic.

A view of the infantry lines at Mena Camp in Egypt, where Roy was briefly trained.

Lone Pine Trench, Gallipoli, with Australian and Turkish dead on the parapet.

A warm day on the Gallipoli Peninsula, 1915. The soldiers, probably British, are swimming after returning from the trenches.

A kitchen in the snow in White Gully, Gallipoli, November 1915, shortly before the evacuation.

A barge containing Gallipoli wounded, alongside the hospital ship Gascon.

An Australian soldier using the famous periscope rifle at Gallipoli, 1915. It had been invented by Lance Corporal (later Sergeant) W.C.B. Beech of the 2nd Battalion.

Australian ambulance men at Bernafay, France, December 1916, carrying their comrades who were suffering from trench feet, to a transport that was to convey them to hospital.

Roy Kyle (second from left) and other members of his trench mortar battery in France loading their gun, the shell of which was called a 'flying pig'.

Standing in a trench in France, 1916, a soldier models the type of gas mask used in the trenches. The wraparound cloth mask featured a carbon filter that removed impurities from the air.

A sprightly Roy Kyle at 97 years of age, as pictured by Steven Siewert in
The Last Anzacs.

pinned down with no hope of advancing and that his order for the 2nd Brigade to mount a bayonet attack and attempt to cross 400 Plateau on their own is pointless and tantamount to suicide. He cannot hope to outflank the Turks, who by now are reinforced and sitting pretty well dug in on the high ground overlooking the plateau. Simple observation shows the plateau scattered with the Anzac dead and the invulnerable Turkish position on the slopes beyond it. The only sensible option is to dig in with the remains of the 9th Battalion and form a front line under the shelter of the reverse slope.

However, a day that has begun with disastrous decisions seems destined to continue in the same way. M'Cay decides to take his men across 400 Plateau and, if he can't get to the Turks with his bayonets, to dig in on the other side. He gives the order to go over the top, and platoon officers, brandishing their Webley revolvers above their heads in some form of battlefield tally-ho, followed by their men with fixed bayonets, pour over the rim of 400 Plateau. In less than half an hour the entire area of the plateau is littered with new corpses in an orgy of killing by the Turks.

Wounded men, abandoning their rifles, attempt to crawl back to the safety of the rim. In the process they are picked off by the Turkish snipers. Often two or three bullets hit a wounded soldier, his body jerking with each impact, before he lies still, sprawled spiderlike, his face against the hard earth, quivering like a rabid dog shot in a suburban street.

The Indian mountain guns are firing willy-nilly into the ridge directly above them and are seemingly as ineffective as a popgun fired at a brick wall, their aim totally random and unco-ordinated, firing at an enemy well dug in. Rifle and machine-gun fire are equally pointless when directing bullets into a blank mountainside at an enemy you can't see. In this respect M'Cay is correct. The only way to get at the Turks is by means of a bayonet charge at close quarters, and there is Buckley's chance of that happening. M'Cay's 2nd Brigade is dying at a much faster rate than during the early-morning slaughter of the 3rd Brigade.

To understand more clearly what was happening, imagine an amphitheatre. The plateau becomes its stage, the hapless Anzacs are the actors and the audience in the seats near the top are the enemy artillery positions from which all movement into every corner of the stage can be covered.

The Turkish gunfire from the ridge is even more concentrated than on the beach and has gained a steady rhythm. Every thirty seconds a salvo of four shells falls, covering a large section of the plateau in the same manner as a moving garden spray might cover a lawn. Two enemy batteries, one at Chunuk Bair in the north and the other at Scrubby

Knoll in the south, prove the deadliest. Depending on where the largest concentration of Australians appear on the plateau, these two batteries immediately shorten or lengthen their range like a fire hose playing on flames so that no single salvo misses its target.

It should have become apparent to M'Cay after the very first troops are sent over the rim that the attempt to get his 2nd Brigade across must fail. He had only to count the dead lying on the plateau from the earlier attempts by the 3rd Brigade to cross to know that there could be no front line to reinforce. Simple arithmetic would have shown that there were too many factors against him to succeed. Colonel M'Cay is wantonly slaughtering his men, thinking only to slavishly obey his misdirected orders. He is unable to accept the responsibility, as senior officer in the field, to call the rescue off. The first rule in the military hand-book is that in a rescue operation you do not sacrifice more men than you hope to save.

Yet, strangely, despite the terrible cost, the young Australian troops after the slaughter of the first few days remain up-beat, too inexperienced to accept defeat, too brave and proud of their heritage and their own ideal of manhood to know when to prudently retreat, confident to the end they would prove superior warriors and that victory must be the inevitable outcome.

The Turks, far from admiring the courage of the Australians, wonder at the stupidity of the infidels and their commanders. They take great heart from what they witness at 400 Plateau. This is an enemy to be laughed at. Even the lowest Turkish recruit knows that stupidity, even brave stupidity, seldom wins battles. Commanders like Colonel M'Cay, who substitute men for ideas and approach a battle with complete disregard for saving the lives of the troops under their command, almost always turn battles into killing fields.

However, the manner of fighting the Turk on the Gallipoli peninsula on the first day by M'Cay sets a pattern for the Australian commanders on several other occasions – Lone Pine, The Nek, the Daisy Patch, German Officer's Trench and Quinn's Post, the latter being where some of the bloodiest and most determined fighting on both sides took place in June 1915. The side that held Quinn's held the key to the beachhead and so both sides crowded into the narrow space until opposing trenches were twenty yards apart at the furthermost point and, incredibly, just two feet apart at the nearest. Dozens of attempts were made on both sides to take the trenches that lay so tantalisingly close to their own. Bayonet charges were frequent, yet none suc-ceeded, each new sortie blown to oblivion by the defending side. In the end the bodies in the intervening space lay piled upon each other rotting in the sun, Muslim embracing Christian, sworn enemies finally reconciled in death. Yet there was no temporary armistice called to remove the dead from No Man's Land. Quinn's Post became the living embodiment of hell itself. Over the months that the stale-mate at Quinn's Post persisted, both sides displayed a degree of grim tenacity and endurance seldom witnessed in warfare. There is a macabre incident told where a soldier crawling back towards his comrades takes a direct hit in the face and blood pours from his nose, mouth, even his eyes, though he can scarcely be seen after a few moments as the flies completely obscure what's left of his features, turning the entire front surface of his smashed and broken head into a blank, black, buzzing horror.

The air in the trenches seemed thick with the stench of rotting corpses, and the plague of swarming flies feeding on the putrefaction carried dysentery and other intestinal maladies to the troops. Despite outbreaks of fly-related disease and other problems caused by a lack of basic hygiene, neither the men nor those in command realised the need for sanitation. By June, the infestation had reached the stage where it became impossible to open one's mouth without swallowing a dozen flies, their bodies bloated from feeding on putrid flesh. What began at Quinn's Post would spread throughout the peninsula and by the end of July the rate of sickness exceeded that of the wounded.

And, of course, there were to be some notable successes among the military failures. On 19 May, the by-now overconfident Turks attempted to throw the Australians back to the beach, but this time the Anzacs had their trenches in place and were in a position to defend their line and some 10,000 of the enemy were killed or wounded.

Private D. Ranford, a Boer War veteran, would later reflect on this particular battle: *'The dead . . . close around our section of the trenches . . . were thick enough to satisfy the most martial, but further along on our right they were in thousands, acres and acres simply covered with them, of course these were mostly Turks when they charged so bravely but were simply mowed down like hay before the mower.'*

It was during the last hours of the Turkish attack in this 19 May battle that a breakthrough arrived via an unexpected quarter which, if it didn't defeat the enemy, it undoubtedly saved countless lives from sniper fire. Major Blamey, who later became General Blamey, the commander in chief of Allied Land Forces in the South-west Pacific area during World War II, walking through the front trench at a point known as the Pimple, observed two men making a framework from planks taken from a supplies box and wire that they had attached to a rifle they were fixing to the parapet. Curious, Blamey asked what they were doing. 'An arrangement so that you can hit without being hit, sir,' one of them explained.

It turned out to be a homemade periscope, a triangular device simply, though ingeniously, attached to a rifle where the upper glass looked along the sights, while the sniper gazed into the lower one situated well below the lip of the parapet. Blamey liked the idea and thought it might be valuable and so arranged for the inventor, Lance Corporal William Charles Bulloch Beech, who in peacetime had been a builder's foreman, to come to headquarters and build several of these rifle periscopes. By 26 May a factory was started on the beach and the first rifle made was taken to Quinn's. The soldier carrying it up to the post got tired of being asked about it by curious troops and took to saying, 'Mate, I'm bloody tired of fightin' Turks; I'm goin' to play them cricket.' In ranges up to 300 yards the periscope rifle was found to be a deadly accurate weapon and it was put to constant use wherever the trenches were close. At Quinn's, where scarcely a shot could be fired during the day without endangering the life of the rifleman, it helped beat down the enemy snipers, who now couldn't understand how they were being picked off without ever glimpsing their opposite number. This simple invention was to give the garrison at Quinn's the eventual superior fire power, which meant that now it was the Turks who found it perilous to show their heads by day over the parapet.

Towards the end of June, those in command seemed at last to come to their senses, men were continuing to die needlessly without any military advantage and it was apparent that the troops were losing faith in their generals. Trench warfare was indecisive, and raids, mostly involving suicidal bayonet attacks, were illustrating the stalemate where neither side could hope for victory. The men saw their mates die without having gained a single initiative over the enemy and they began, for the first time, to doubt the victory they had promised themselves. In between these deadly skirmishes, the troops were confined to the trenches for long periods without a break. In the eyes of the men the war had become short sharp bursts of unnecessary killing followed by long, deeply monotonous periods in which they became bored and sick. Bad food and constant dehydration taxed their strength. They lived on a frugal and inadequate diet, mostly iron rations, and received a third of a gallon of water per day for all purposes. In addition to fighting and digging, they were expected to carry their own supplies and assume fatigues not usually the tasks of front-line troops. One in eight were assigned to carrying water up the steep slopes, others manufactured bombs or worked in burial parties. With dysentery reaching epidemic proportions, half the men on the peninsula were sick and the remainder perpetually exhausted so that none were equal to the strain of prolonged battle.

July proved to be a relatively quiet month with the Anzacs maintaining their positions without any major battles or even skirmishes taking place. New recruits filling the trenches to replace the sick and the dead soon grew bored and hungered for the kind of battle the old soldiers spoke of in their seemingly glorious past. These young men, unlike their now seasoned and disillusioned comrades in arms, still harboured visions of martial glory and resented the tedium of the trenches. They were not yet weak with the effects of dysentery, dehydration or malnutrition and complained that it wasn't a war at all, for they saw few dead and wounded and heard only an occasional rifle shot in the distance or an artillery shell whiz overhead to explode into the mountainside above them. They longed for a chance to fix bayonets and to show the enemy they were true blue and would accept nothing less than a victorious outcome as their birthright.

Their time finally came in late July when the Australian battalions were told that they were to undertake another general assault. It was 'whacko, 'ere we go!' for the new-comers and, for the old-timers, the calm resignation that they would once again have to trust to the fortunes of war. God would point His finger and, having pointed, move on to some other bloke who would wonder for the remainder of his life why he had been spared while his mate beside him had copped a Turkish bullet through the heart.

The task allotted to the Australians during August was to act as feints, the idea being to decoy Turkish reserves away from Suvla Bay, north of Anzac, where 25,000 British New Army troops were to land and mount an assault at daybreak on 7 August. The first of these 'feints', which the Australians and New Zealanders took as major enterprises and which, indeed, they turned out to be, was to take place just before sunset on the evening before the British landing. It was to be against the Turkish trenches at a place initially named Lonesome Pine after a popular song at the time and eventually shortened to Lone Pine, a name forever redolent in Antipodean history of courage, tenacity and great sacrifice. In fact the pine tree after which the battlefield was known had long since become a casualty of war, taking several hits from artillery and mortar fire so that at the time of the assault it had become a shredded stump. The distance to the Turkish trenches was some eighty yards over largely open ground covered with juniper and scrub, which the Turks slashed to a height of roughly three feet near their own trenches, while the rest of the area was criss-crossed with barbed wire. For the Australians, the taking and holding of Lone Pine was to prove the bloodiest and most sustained fighting of the entire Gallipoli campaign.

The battle was expected to be hand-to-hand and unremitting, as holding Lone Pine was thought to be critical to both sides. As the fighting would take place in the late afternoon and during dusk, the Australian troops wore white calico patches sewn to their backs and sleeves so that they could be distinguished from the Turk in the approaching darkness. By two-thirty, they had stacked their packs for later recovery and filed into the trenches facing the pine eighty yards away, one company from each attacking battalion taking their place. At four o'clock, the allied artillery began the softening-up process, bombarding the Turkish trenches. The battle had begun and it wasn't long before the Turkish artillery replied. Here is a description of that moment by Private McAnulty of the 2nd Battalion, formally a clerk from Melbourne: *'There [sic] artillery are replying now & shells are beginning to rain on us. They are getting the range now, shelling the support trenches. Men are beginning to drop. Howitzer shells are dropping about 30 yards from us digging great holes where they land, the fumes are suffocating, the shrapnel is pouring all round us getting chaps everywhere. This is hell waiting here . . .'*

By 5.30 p.m., with the sun now low enough to be shining directly into the eyes of the waiting Turks, the whistles blew and the Anzacs poured out of their trenches.

'The next thing was charge. (oh mummer). The Turks poured machine gun fire, Artillery, shrapnell shells, and Bombs, rifle fire, Lydite, and the Lord only knows what into us . . .' Corporal R. P. Brett, 2nd Battalion, labourer of Sydney.

Later, seated in a captured Turkish trench, Private McAnulty wrote in his notebook:

I've pulled through alright so far, just got a few minutes to spare now. I'm all out, can hardly stand up. On Friday when we got the word to charge Frank & I were on the extreme left of the charging party. There was a clear space of 100 yards to cross without a patch of cover. I can't realise how I got across it, I seemed to be in a sort of trance. The rifle & machine gun fire was hellish. I remember dropping down when we reached their trenches, looked around & saw Frank & 3 other men alongside me. There was a big gap between us & and the rest of the men . . .

> [who] were right out in the open . . . I yelled out to
> the other 4 chaps, 'This is suicide boys, I'm going
> to make a jump for it.' I thought they said alright we'll
> follow. I sprang to my feet in one jump . . .'

At that moment, while writing, he was killed. Corporal
McAnulty was one of thousands who died at Lone Pine,
which was to continue long past the initial taking of the
Turkish trenches on that first day. The purpose was not
only to hold the trenches but to provoke counterattacks
designed to absorb the Turkish reserves. If they failed in
this task, then the battle for Lone Pine would be largely
pointless. The British High Command had hoped to
embroil at least two Turkish regiments in the attempt
to retake Lone Pine. The Australians were so successful at
the distraction that they attracted an additional enemy
division.

The first counterattack by the Turks came on the night
of 6 August and would last for three days, when wave after
wave of soldiers hurled themselves at the Australian
defences. It was the same kind of insanity witnessed by
the Turks on the first day of landing on 400 Plateau, only
this time it was in reverse.

The newcomers, who a short time before lamented the
fact that they had come too late for the fighting, found

themselves with fixed bayonet, up to their armpits in blood and gore, fighting off the Turkish assault. Crude hand grenades, known at the time as bombs, which contained an explosive in a round container the size of a cricket ball, would be lit and hurled into the trenches by the Turks. It took several seconds for the fuse to burn down and explode and the Australians would catch them and hurl them back over the parapet often losing a hand or, worse, their lives in the process. Sometimes, if they could reach it on time, they'd throw a blanket over the bomb and allow it to explode harmlessly at their feet.

The Australians replied with homemade bombs made from jam tins filled with guncotton and bark wire pieces. There was never a moment to think and the men fought until they dropped from exhaustion, unable to rise up from their knees. Still the battle raged on.

For three days there was hardly a moment's rest, and in the words of Private W. Bendrey: '[The dead] *were lying everywhere, on top of the parapet . . . in dugouts & communication trenches and saps, and it was impossible to avoid treading on them. In the second line the Turkish dead were lying everywhere, and if a chap wanted to sit down for a spell he was often compelled to squat on one of 'em.'*

Another soldier simply known as De Vine, his rank unknown, said: '*The stench of the dead bodies now is simply awfull, as they have been fully exposed to the sun for several days, many have swollen terribly and have burst . . . many men wear gas protectors [against the stench] . . . there has been no attempt up to the present to either remove or bury [the dead], they are stacked out of the way in any convenient place sometimes thrown up on to the parados so as not to block up the trenches, there are more dead than living . . . [and] we have been too busy to do anything in the matter.'* De Vine was killed three days into the battle and not long before the Turks, at last realising that the main threat to them lay elsewhere, began to withdraw.

On 9 August, the Turks had had enough. They had lost more than 6000 men in the three days of fighting and had used up most of their reserves. Australia, too, had required additional troops and had sent the 12th and the 7th Battalions into the breach where they soon became part of the decimation and, in the end, the generals were forced to further add the 7th Light Horse Regiment and elements of the 5th Battalion. It was said at the time that no army could have asked more from their men, who had fought beyond the normal capacity of men at arms. At Lone Pine, 2300 Australians were killed or wounded and about half the packs stacked before the battle were never claimed. Those who had owned them lay at Lone Pine where they still lie today. When the burial parties were at last able to get to the men, they swept up the maggots dropping from the dead by the bucketful. Lone Pine was where the legend of Gallipoli was finally consolidated. This place, where a scraggy windswept pine once stood, would be spoken of in awe by Australians ever afterwards.

Lone Pine wasn't the only battle in which the Australians were called on to fight. On 6 August, the evening after the capture of Lone Pine, the 4th Brigade, along with the New Zealanders and the Indians and some elements of the main British attacking force, were given the task to gain the heights approaching Hill 971. These heights looked over the Dardanelles and the position would also secure the southern flank of the English at Suvla. They were the key to the peninsula and could well make victory for the allies possible. The feint at Lone Pine had worked a treat and the Turks were pouring their reserves into retaking their captured trenches, which, in effect, left the heights along Hill 971 exposed. The proposition was for the New Zealanders, Indians and the 4th Brigade to advance as soon as night fell and, during the night, occupy the heights. It was a good plan and had every chance of working but for one thing, no one knew the way through the rough and scrubby country with its numerous small dead-end valleys and dark gullies. Advancing in the dark without lights to guide them, they soon became confused and started to fall behind in what was a very narrow window of opportunity where they must be in control of the heights by dawn or it would be too late.

Daylight arrived with no unit having reached its objective. The men, wearied by a night of toil and weakened by months of sickness, were simply not up to the struggle the hostile terrain presented. The New Zealanders were closest and on this occasion, the Australians, suffering from confused leadership, had fallen the furtherst behind.

There was still a chance to succeed, as the Turkish reserves, normally positioned on the heights, had been called to Lone Pine without having been replaced. However, the Kiwis weren't aware of this and stopped for breakfast. It was a reasonable call, the men were exhausted, but it is precisely those times in war when men are called to respond beyond their normal will which lead to victory. While their leaders debated the situation, the Turks saw what was happening and sent reinforcements from The Nek. The New Zealanders finally attacked Chunuk Bair a mile and a half from Hill 971 at 11 a.m. and occupied it for a short time before the Turkish reinforcements successfully repelled their attack. Hill 971 was one of the few times in the Gallipoli campaign where Australians did not acquit themselves well and where they showed a lack of their customary grit and character.

If Lone Pine, with 2300 men dead or wounded, could

be said to have been a great victory, then the remaining feints that took place on 7 August, must equally be called disasters:

- Three hundred men of the 6th Battalion attacked German Officer's Trench, losing 146 men without success.
- The 1st Light Horse Regiment with 200 men successfully occupied the trenches on Dead Man's Ridge but were driven out again with 154 casualties.
- Fifty-four troopers of the 2nd Light Horse Regiment attacked Turkish Quinn's and all but one lost their lives.

These three extremely gallant attacks, where the men were greatly outnumbered, achieved almost nothing.

However, the most tragic and sacrificial feint was made by the 8th and 10th Light Horse Regiments at The Nek, from where earlier in the day the Turkish reinforcements that repelled the New Zealanders at Chunuk Bair had been despatched. It was here where a seven-minute delay cost the lives of almost every member of the two regiments.

I wrote about this assault in my introduction but it is worth expanding upon, if only as an example of the extreme gallantry of men who will persist when the odds are hopelessly stacked against them. In retrospect we may think of the proposed feint against The Nek as extremely stupid but, it must be remembered, this was a different time when the heads of young boys were filled with the derring-do of sacrifice to King and the British Empire and when the charge of the Light Brigade during the not-too-distant Crimean War was the stuff of which true Englishmen were made. For their part, the young Australians needed to prove themselves even more intrepid than their antecedents, so that they too might qualify to be included in the pantheon of the illustrious dead.

The attack on The Nek was a well-planned operation to be given all the pertinence of a major assault. It is important to imagine a battleground which was about the width of a football pitch at the Anzac line and then narrowed to about the length, perhaps just a little more, of a tennis court at the Turkish front. In fact it was a tiny place but, worse still, the trenches of either side were just twenty yards apart, less than the distance a kid can throw a stone. Five Turkish machine guns covered the intervening ground so that not an inch remained beyond the reach of their metal-tipped bullets. The Turks were well dug in what was a slightly uphill run for the attacking Australians.

The charge would be preceded by a naval and artillery bombardment, which began at four o'clock on the afternoon of 6 August and it was planned to continue for the next twelve hours and thirty minutes exactly, when the first 150 men in the first trench would go over the top and, with bayonet and rifle, charge the Turkish trenches. Alas, due probably to the simple maladjustment of someone's watch, the bombardment stopped seven minutes short. Seven minutes in twelve hours does not seem like a lot of time but to the Turks who had kept their heads down, unable to man their machine guns for twelve hours and twenty-three minutes, it was sufficient time to emerge from deep shelter and to fire in short bursts to clear their machine guns and man their rifles. At precisely four-thirty, just as dawn broke, the first line of the 8th Light Horse leapt from their trenches. Their sun helmets had hardly appeared above the parapets when the first of them were mowed down. The line kept coming but was decimated within the first five yards. One or two Australians managed to cover the twenty yards to the enemy trenches before being killed, while the remainder lay on or near the lip of their own trenches dead or mortally wounded.

Clearly, the situation was hopeless and it was pointless to continue the attack. The Turks were completely in control and the firepower of the five machine guns they had in place was more than sufficient to mow down any frontal attack. The second line waiting in the trenches saw their mates die. The sound of the Turkish gunfire over their heads was horrendous, like the clatter of hail on a tin roof. At their feet lay some of their dead comrades who hadn't even made it out of the trench. It was time to pull out.

But that's not what happened. They waited the required two minutes as ordered, then they too rushed forward and immediately died to a man. The 10th Light Horse moved into the places their now dead mates had vacated moments before, and they knew they must die. *'Boys, you have ten minutes to live,'* their commanding officer, Lt Col. J. W. Springthorpe shouted, *'and I am going to lead you.'* The men shook hands with their mates, took position, and when the order came they went over the top to be slaughtered, every one of them. Someone tried to halt the fourth line but in the noise and confusion of battle they too climbed out to die beside their comrades. Two hundred and thirty-four light horsemen lay dead. It was now 5.15, with the sun just peeking up behind the heights.

Somehow, The Nek was to become a symbol not just for Gallipoli but for the Great War, where men were slaughtered in great numbers while others looked on seemingly unconcerned. The English troops at Suvla, plainly visible from The Nek, were making tea while the Australians willingly sacrificed their lives. Their gallantry will never be forgotten, but the stupidity of their commanding generals must never be forgiven. This was a war where too many of the beautiful young of every nation were sacrificed willy-nilly by old men smelling of whisky, with the brass buttons on their tunics stretched to breaking point over their paunches. Dyspeptic colonels and generals, spluttering and mumbling through their tobacco-stained moustaches, watched men die through the rubber eyepieces of their field glasses and pronounced the battles glorious.

The second stage of the Gallipoli campaign was over, and with it, most of the fighting. It was at this stage that Roy Kyle arrived and it here that his story takes up.

Early in the morning of the next day – the fifth – a Sunday during which the Turks were indulging in a demonstration of thousands of rifles blazing away at nothing in particular. We were taken ashore on barges lashed to the sides of small, powered boats of the Royal Navy and disembarked at Watson's Pier, a small, ramshackle affair but the only pier on Anzac Beach at that time. A second smaller one was later built despite the attention of 'Beachy Bill', a Turkish gun or guns, which enfiladed the beach and defied all efforts of the R.N. to destroy them. 'C' company, of which I was a member, was given the job of unloading the stores, most of which were stacked at the end of the pier, and my platoon (12) was placed on guard over them.

It was here that I had my first experience of fire. 'Beachy Bill', delighted at the activity, shelled us constantly while we huddled behind the boxes, mainly of ammunition, but, lucky for us, did not register a hit, although he was horribly close at times. The stores were moved to safer cover as the day wore on and we moved up on one of the gullies – Steeles', I think – and bivouacked on a grassy knoll (Pluggs Plateau) one of the few reasonably level spots I ever saw on the Peninsula.

I didn't make friends easily and the crowded army life, with its complete lack of privacy, did not make it any easier. In any case, I had been with the unit only twelve or fourteen days. The great majority had trained together in Australia and Egypt and close friendships had been formed and outsiders were not particularly welcomed. True, I had formed casual acquaintanceships with several men of 12 Platoon but they, too, had their established connections and I was too diffident to make approaches. Many, I think, must have wondered at my withdrawn attitude but hesitated to intrude. They were a mixed bunch drawn from all grades of society, from the vicious to the evangelical, from the back-street fighter to the academic, from the timid to the braggart, and many, like me, of no particular group or grouping. Completely alone, I lay down on the ground and tried to sleep.

That night, I remember, was clear with the stars shining brightly. Sleep was slow in coming and was not helped by the Turk turning on a 'demonstration'. The hubbub having subsided I eventually fell into an uneasy sleep, only to be awakened sometime later by one of the most terrifying experiences of my life. Sometime in the morning – my guess is about two or three o'clock – I woke with a sharp pain in my left groin. I had unbuttoned my pants and tunic for comfort, and on reaching down my hand groped something soft and yielding. I dragged it away from the hold it had on me and with a convulsive effort hurled it far into the darkness. I was close to panic. I was within two months of my eighteenth birthday, far away from home and country, amongst an army of men, not one of them whom I could call my friend, with enemy rifles blazing away with their bullets towards me and those around me, and the occasional boom of guns firing, followed a few seconds later by the blast of a bursting shell much closer. I resisted the panic and started to wonder what it was that had fastened on to me and what I should do about it. Was it a field mouse or small rat, a vampire bat or a scorpion? I discarded the last as it felt too compact and yielding, and if it was either of the first two no great harm had been done. In any case, there was little I could do. I supposed the battalion had a doctor attached, but I had not seen or heard of one and had no chance of finding him. The only thing to do was to await developments, hope for the best and try to go to sleep which proved to be impossible.

I suffered no ill effects other than the aftermath of a bad scare which remained with me for the rest of the night and following day. The memory still haunts me, more I think, than the memory of bad times which followed on Gallipoli and in France.

We moved into the trenches at Steele's Post the following day. The trenches were deep and dry and there was little action from the enemy, who appeared to be a couple of hundred yards away. After two days we moved to Lone Pine, which was to be our holding position for the rest of our time on the Peninsula.

The men of the 1st Division, whom we relieved, were a fair sample of the survivors . . . They were half-starved, gaunt, grubby – and confident. Nothing could lower their morale or defeat those men.

Lone Pine has been written about perhaps more than any single place or event, other than the landing during the Gallipoli campaign . . . The Turk had many attempts to recapture it but all had been repulsed. It was thought that he would renew his attempts, but as was later learned, his losses had been so heavy as to discourage him. Consequently, we were in a holding position during the almost four months we were there. That, however, was no sinecure . . . Our foothold on the peninsula was precarious indeed.

Nothing could be more primitive than the living conditions. At White's Valley the ground was of a chalky nature and men in their twos, threes and fours dug out and into the side of the valley areas large enough for their separate needs. These they roofed with waterproof sheets or, in time, with galvanised iron if they were fortunate enough to come by such a treasure, by whatever means.

A loner, but pleasant chap, named Landers suggested that we form a team, to which I readily agreed, and we dug out an area with entrenching tools, which was to be our 'home', when out of the trenches, for our stay on the peninsula.

We were an ill-matched pair. He was a farmer, a silent man of about thirty-five, but a good fellow who never made me feel the difference in our ages. We became good, but never close, friends. We were in different platoons and never saw each other when in the line and that was the place where close friendships were made. After leaving the peninsula, I do not remember ever seeing him again.

The food was deplorable and consisted mainly of tinned bullybeef and hardtack biscuits about four inches square which broke more teeth than teeth broke biscuits. When in the line, this was supplemented by bullybeef stew, which was repulsive, and rice and raisins swimming in hot water, obtained from the cooks. Jam, mostly plum or plum and apple, was also issued to be eaten on the biscuits. A mug of black tea (with Nestle's condensed milk, if you were lucky enough to have received a parcel from home) was also issued. I remember only once, possibly twice, being issued with bread during our stay. Our diet in the trenches and the saps was supplemented by sugar bags of currants.

I occupied post No. 5 in the line with a Ballarat man, 'Flash Jack' Webb. His nickname was misleading, due more to the jauntiness with which he wore his hat than to any other reason. He was killed within a yard of me on 23 September, three weeks after we occupied Lone Pine. The trenches were deep and dry and as safe as a trench could be twenty to twenty-five yards from the trenches of a bomb-throwing enemy, except for one thing, a loophole which was a death trap. The firing steps were areas large enough to accommodate two men, carved out about two to three feet above the bottom of the trench with the front and sides surrounded by sandbags. The death trap was in the steel plate, with a loophole in its centre, embedded in the sandbags facing the Turk. He had a supply of vicious high-velocity German field guns, and if one of his shells hit the steel plate it turned into shrapnel. I had stepped down into the trench to retrieve the remains of a blanket we had thrown over a bomb that had landed on our fire step and which we had kicked into the trench (each post was equipped with a blanket or old greatcoat for the purpose). They probably, to some extent, dampened down the explosion. Jack had his rifle through the loophole, through which he was looking, in the hope of spotting the Turk who had thrown the bomb, when a shell from one of the field guns hit the plate. The result was horrific and Jack died instantly. I, miraculously, was not scratched.

The four main pests which made life almost impossible on Gallipoli were flies, lice, rats and Turks, in that order. Flies swarmed everywhere and it was a continual fight to keep them out of food, mouth and eyes. You would try with one hand to move them off as you put food into your mouth, but almost invariably some got through. Rats were everywhere; they were repulsive but you got used to them. Lice, like flies, attacked viciously and in large numbers, congregating in the seams of underclothes. You could kill them between your thumbnails by the hundreds but in an hour or two they would be back as thick as ever. The Turk was the least of the pests. True, he was continually trying to kill us and we were trying to kill him, yet it was remarkable what little hard feeling there was against him. I am sure we would have been good friends had we met under normal conditions, as was proven when the madness eventually ended. He had a great sense of humour and would gaily wave a miss with his spade whenever we fired at him while he was deepening his trenches.

Periscope attachments for our rifles were introduced and proved to be a lifesaver. Although the Turk continually broke the mirrors in the periscopes, we no longer had to poke a rifle through a loophole, which he was always quick to spot and take a quick shot at with disastrous results should you be sighting your rifle. The periscope decreased accuracy but you seldom had a definite target so that did not much matter.

From No. 5, my habitual post, we had a definite target and a clear view of a string of Turks always going or coming on the one line. We did not know what it was all about but, by trial and error with the periscope rifle, we finally arrived, by the way the Turks accelerated when we fired, at the range of 800 yards. We had great fun, although I doubt if we ever hit anyone. We were ordered to stop when the company sniper, who had a lair at the back of the trench just above us, complained that we were ruining his best target, and that the traffic was on a path to a latrine hidden from our view. The sniper was Corporal Stan Savige, Lieutenant-General Sir Stanley Savige of Second World War fame, his last active command being, I think, Commander-in-Chief of Australian forces in New Guinea. In civilian life he was one of the founders of Legacy in Australia, after seeing the Remembrance Club operating in Tasmania.

In most places on the battalion front, the trenches were within bomb-throwing distance of each other. Fortunately, the length of the Turkish fuse usually gave you time to kick it off the firing step if it landed there, and throw an old blanket or trench coat over it, but sometimes an adventurous Turk would hold the grenade for a few seconds before throwing it, in which case you were lucky if it missed your firing step and landed outside the trench.

The Turk's main short-range weapon was his broomstick mortar bomb. It was a cylinder about twelve inches in diameter by about eighteen inches long, attached to a steel rod three to four inches thick by four to five feet in length, which fitted into the mortar barrel and became a whirling menace when the bomb exploded. All the mortar bomb needed was a witch with a broom and a peaked hat astride it. The bombs were seldom aimed at the trenches as they were inaccurate and the trenches at Lone Pine were too close for safety. Brown's Dip, about 200 yards behind the line, which accommodated cooks, stores etc, was a favourite target. Fortunately, the bombs flew high in the air and a lookout could be kept for them.

We worked with the 23rd Battalion on a two-days-in, two-days-out basis, the latter usually devoted to fatigue duty, such as digging saps or carrying stores up to the various parts of the line. When in the trenches, it was two hours on post and four off. 'Off' meant retiring a few yards, sitting down to write or delouse or lying down to rest and sleep, if one could find a place where it was safe to do so without being trodden on.

A problem was keeping as clean as conditions would

allow. The only way to do so was to run the gauntlet with Beachy Bill and take a dip in the Aegean. You learnt to be cunning about this by waiting undercover until the water was as free of bathers as it was likely to become, since Johnny Turk would not be as trigger-happy if the target was just two or three bathers.

Shaving was also a problem and the lathering was usually done with the aid of a small quantity of tea left in the bottom of a mess tin. Needless to say, it was accomplished only at irregular and well-spaced intervals.

Boredom often set in despite the steady killing and wounding and evacuation of the sick and wounded. There was no entertainment, no kiosks of any sort, and no evidence that there had ever been any habitation in the area; that was all on the narrows mostly on the opposite shore – our unobtainable goal.

We had two pays of one pound each whilst on the peninsula and they produced frantic gambling at cards, crown and anchor, and two-up until the money – or ninety per cent of it – found its way into one pocket.

Everything we ate, drank, wore or fired had to be brought by sea. Drinking water was the main problem and, in an effort to relieve the situation, a condensing unit was built on the beach. Beachy Bill promptly pumped a shell into it and, for some days, the only water we had was one pint per man per day issued to the cooks for cooking and tea-making. It was during this period that C Company, on fatigue through Shrapnel Gully, rushed the water tanks there. They were under armed guard, but to the everlasting credit of the men on guard, they refrained from using their rifles. The position remained ugly for a while but the men were eventually persuaded by their officers to continue their fatigue and no great harm was done.

On 29 November, while the 24th was relieving the 23rd Battalion, the Turk opened fire with an intensity not previously experienced. He had acquired heavy howitzers and these and heavy guns from warships in the Narrows, plus the customary array of howitzers and field guns, were turned onto the small Lone Pine salient with devastating effect. During the night the Turk had placed small red flags along their trenches, no doubt to direct their gun fire – although the troops had jokingly claimed that 'Johnny is going to hold a race meeting'. We were on territory which three months before had been occupied by them and they knew the position of every sap, tunnel and trench. Consequently, their first shots closed the entries to the tunnels (built by them) leading from Brown's Dip to the front line, which was almost obliterated, filling in the entrances to numerous dugouts and trapping literally hundreds of men. Number 12 platoon had reached a dugout, just behind the front line, running about twelve or fifteen feet into the wall of the sap, and we had leant our rifles against the inner wall and deposited surplus gear, when a shell blast closed the entrance and we were trapped.

It was bitterly cold. A blizzard, with a heavy fall of snow having raged for the previous couple of days and nights, made it difficult. When we broke out, meeting those who were digging from the other side, the bolts on our rifles were frozen, although we did not know that until we tried to fire them.

Immediately after being freed, I was ordered to my usual No. 5 post, which was one of the few positions which had escaped destruction. On looking through the loophole, I discovered a very large-headed Turk, head and shoulders above the trench, twenty-five yards away from me and directly in front. Instead of being elated, I was distressed. I had fired at many Turks from a distance without knowing if I had hit them, but this was different. I could not miss him and it seemed more like murder than warfare. In the early 1900s the stress in sport – particularly in the schools – was on 'fair play'. 'The great thing in life is not to win the game but to play a bad hand well' is a morbid cliché today, but the sentiment it expressed was drummed into us with almost religious fervour. (*Tom Brown's Schooldays* was a favourite boys' book.)

The Turk looked to be a man of thirty and probably had a wife and kids back home in Turkey, but if I let him go he might kill me or my friends. All these things ran through my mind but I decided I had to shoot him and forced myself, as quietly as possible, to put the end of my rifle barrel through the loophole and take aim. A mixture of raw cold and dirt had affected the firing mechanism of my rifle and the only response when I pulled the trigger was a faint click. Faint as it was, he heard it and disappeared in a flash. My relief was great but was somewhat short-lived as he immediately threw a bomb which, fortunately, landed short and exploded harmlessly a yard or two from the parapet. I threw one in reply, which I thought to be more accurate.

Nothing changed much. I had my eighteenth birthday

on 9 November. The sunsets over Imbros continued their beautiful display, and we continued to wonder how we could ever make it to the island if the impossible happened and, by sheer weight of numbers, we were pushed back the few hundred yards to the sea. Field Marshal Lord Kitchener (Commander-in-Chief of the British Army) came and went. Very few saw him and we had no inkling that he had decided on evacuation. However, we soon knew that something was in the air as strange things began to happen, and presaged that we were commencing preparations for evacuation. The possibility of such a move had been talked about for some time as it was obvious that, inadequately clothed, fed and acclimatised, we would have great difficulty in holding on during a bitter winter.

Roy Kyle was a product of his time when it simply wasn't done to boast of one's achievements. While this is something we can all admire, it isn't always useful in the telling of a story. Roy was one of the last hundred soldiers to leave the beach and, while he eventually did so safely, this was never anticipated. It was always considered probable the Turks would catch on to what was happening and that there would be an attrition rate of up to twenty-five per cent. The troops who largely organised the evacuation from the beach and elsewhere would almost inevitably have to be sacrificed, a statistic pretty well known to everyone. Volunteers were called for and Kyle put up his hand. Under the circumstances it was an extremely brave thing to do and, of course, he makes no mention of this in his memoirs.

There is yet another example of Australian ingenuity that took place in the last few days of the evacuation and one that must compare with the periscope rifle, in that it undoubtedly helped to save a great many lives at Gallipoli. For a second time the inspiration came from a lowly lance corporal, only one rank above private.

Twenty-year-old Lance Corporal Scurry, a new arrival on Gallipoli and therefore not subject to the vicissitudes suffered by the vast majority of the Anzacs on the penin-sula, made up for the absence of his fighting contribution in what must surely rate as one of the most brazen pieces of trickery ever perpetuated in warfare. With the help of his Moonee Ponds (Melbourne) schoolmate, 'Buntie' Lawrence, he invented what was to become known vari-ously as the Scurry 'pop-off' rifle, an automatic firing device known more officially as the self-firing rifle.

Scurry's self-firing rifle, like so many original ideas, was absurdly simple yet totally effective. It consisted of two bullybeef tins, of which there was an endless supply, a plank for a packing case, a handful of medium-sized stones and a short length of string. The sketch opposite will better illustrate how it worked. One container, the top one, had a hole at its bottom of various sizes, depending on when the rifle was intended to fire, and was filled with water, which dropped into an empty container directly beneath it. This bottom tin was also attached to a small box of stones. A piece of string was attached to the bottom bullybeef can, and from there to the trigger of the rifle. The bottom container, together with the stones, was delicately balanced on the end of the plank. When the water dripping into the bottom tin reached a certain level, it tipped over, together with the stones, pulling the string around the trigger sufficiently taut to fire the rifle which, in turn, was held down by sandbags and faced the enemy trenches. Simple as that.

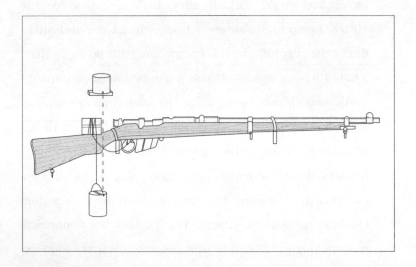

It was decided to adopt this inanely simple device during the evacuation, and to help fool the enemy three days of comparative silence was observed, with only an occasional shot being fired, three weeks before the evacuation. The idea was for the Turks to assume that an evacuation was taking place and to persuade them to attack, only to find the allies in place and ready to take them on. The Turks weren't going to fall for such an unsophisticated trick and they kept their powder dry, so to speak. When three weeks later the same thing happened, the silence only interrupted by an occasional rifle shot, they thought it a simple case of déjà vu and sat back smugly as the Anzacs quietly made their exit.

The result was beyond the highest expectations and fooled the whole Turkish army, making it possible for 100,000 men to 'sneak' away from Anzac Cove and Suvla under the very nose of the enemy and with no more than a handful of casualties. It was a truly extraordinary ruse.

Although it may be said that the leadership at Gallipoli never reached the quality of the men who fought there, with Hamilton being the only high-ranking officer not to be sacked for incompetence, there were a handful of exceptions, Monash, the young Australian Brigadier General being one of them. The Dardanelles Campaign was one huge and terrible mistake, with disaster following disaster. Very few commanders emerged with their reputations intact, but one Australian staff officer, Lieutenant Colonel Brudenell White, left the shores of Gallipoli covered in glory. White was given the responsibility of organising the evacuation, which has often since been described as faultless, a masterpiece, a most brilliant conception, and several dozen other superlatives. Certainly, the withdrawal with only two casualties was unimaginable and, put into the simplest of terms, a miracle.

Scurry wrote about how scared he was at the prospect of being one of the very last to leave Lady Galway Road, the name of the trench system where he was to start operating the self-firing rifles: *'I stood alone in that black tunnel for 15 minutes. White moonlight through the entrances to the rifle possies made it all the more gruesome, and it was a very frightened lad who at last started to fill the water cans . . . Had we only realised that directing the operation was the clearest and most efficient brain that had ever operated under a khaki hat – that of General [sic] White – and that we ourselves were as near perfect in battle discipline as soldiers had ever been, there would have been no worry.'*

There is a small point of parochial interest in the evacuation. The escaping Anzacs were made to wrap strips of torn blanket around their feet to muffle the sound of the mass departure. They termed this clumsy footwear 'sneakers', as in 'sneaking away', and the word was subsequently adopted into the language to describe a soft canvas shoe.

Roy Kyle remained a private throughout the war and his story is about ordinary blokes in extraordinary circumstances, but there cannot be too many instances where the ingenuity of two lance corporals – that of Scurry and Beech – had such a profound effect on an outcome in a time of war.

Scurry's self-firing rifle undoubtedly saved thousands of lives and while it is easy to be overly jingoistic when writing about the exploits of one's country at war, it does seem amazing that the ideas of two common soldiers were so readily accepted by those in command. It is perhaps a good illustration of the egalitarian and easygoing attitude between private and officer of Australians at the time. It is difficult to see how in the British army, with its traditional military dichotomy of rank from file, ideas such as these would have permeated to the top. For instance, the periscope rifle was offered to the English troops at Suvla, where it was politely received but never really put into use.

Scurry, on the other hand, wasn't overlooked. He was promoted to sergeant, mentioned in despatches, awarded the D.C.M. and shortly afterwards was given his commission. In Europe he was made captain in the 15th Light Trench Mortar Battery, which he started from scratch and where, after his success in action at Fromelles, he was subsequently awarded the M.C.

In his capacity as an expert with mortars he was brought the fuse of a German mortar known as a 'Rum Jar', which had failed to explode and appeared to have an unusual fuse. Scurry proceeded to strip the fuse and reassemble it but, as he was replacing the detonator, the striker dropped and he lost an eye and a finger and received wounds to his face and chest. Brigadier General 'Pompey' Elliott, his brigade commander, said when he received news of the accident: *'He was the best and most enthusiastic officer in my Brigade, without exception, and his loss to the Trench Mortar Battery is incalculable. I'd rather have him with one eye than a dozen others with two. In my opinion he is a military genius of a type unfortunately only too rare.'*

Captain Scurry, no longer fit for active service, was made an instructor at the 1st Anzac Corps School at Aveluy where, almost immediately, he was made chief instructor to the 5th Divisional Wing, which included training the American troops in mortar warfare.

It would be tempting to speculate that Roy Kyle, who reached Europe at around the same time as Scurry and, shortly afterwards, was transferred to a mortar battery, might have served under or at least been instructed by this remarkable young Australian officer. However, Kyle makes no mention of this in his memoirs and so it seems unlikely.

E vacuation would be a hazardous operation, with the probability of heavy casualties; no one wanted to leave. There was no sense of defeat and even if we did leave, it would be of our own free will, not because of any pressure by the Turk. In later years it was accepted that Gallipoli was a defeat, but one should feel great pride for the great and courageous effort of the Anzacs and the British and French at Cape Helles.

The evacuation preparations were designed to hoodwink the Turk and, with this end in view, we commenced periods of 'silent warfare' in November. This consisted of complete silence from us for varying times at irregular periods. The times could be one, two or more hours and, once, it extended to two days.

Parties were moving away quietly after dark for several days prior to the final evacuation on the nights of 18 and 19 December.

To deaden the noise of departing troops on the final days and nights, bags, old blankets and greatcoats – in fact anything that would deaden sound were laid down in the trenches and saps. The purpose of the 'silent warfare' stunts became obvious. It was hoped that Johnny Turk's listening posts would fail to pick up the noise of movement and put the silence down to one of our stunts, although he would be rather puzzled by the steady, if spaced, firing from the trenches. This was brought about by men patrolling the line and firing from here and there, and sometimes throwing a bomb – we had recently had our first issue of Mills bombs – to create the illusion of fully manned trenches. The illusion was maintained after completion of the evacuation by the arrangement of two cans of water to fixed rifles, one full of water with a small hole in the bottom above the firing line, the other empty, attached to the trigger . . .

The first party left shortly after dusk and there were several at intervals until early in the morning of the 19th. I was in B2 party, which left from B5 tunnel at 11 p.m. and arrived and embarked at Watson's Pier on a small powered boat about an hour later.

The same thing was happening all along the front, times co-ordinated for all to arrive at, or close to, the same time. Everything, for once, went without a hitch.

The departure of the B2 party left less than a hundred men and N.C.O.s and a handful of officers manning the battalion front usually manned by several hundred.

We were transhipped by Jacob's Ladder to a destroyer, which was packed like sardines in a tin and, before we were out of sight of land on our way to Lemnos, had the pleasures of seeing and hearing the vast conflagration on the beach as the dump of ammunition and stores was blown up by delayed fuse. We knew that the evacuation had been completed. The Turk also knew it, but too late.

It was a magnificent piece of organisation, due mainly to the officer on General Birdwood's staff known later as Lieutenant General Sir Brudenell White, one of the ablest soldiers Australia has produced. He was assisted by the officer who later became Field Marshal Sir Thomas Blamey.

Gallipoli was a failure, a case of 'too little too late'. Had it been carried through with sufficient strength, and less signalling of our intentions, in the first instance it would have shortened the war very considerably (some experts have calculated by as much as eighteen months), and possibly headed off the Russian Revolution long enough for some commonsense to have entered the heads of the ruling class; but that was doubtful.

In the end, seven months after the first shot sounded in the pitch dark at Anzac beach, 240,000 men will have been wounded and over 40,000 killed on the Allied side. The Turks never counted their dead, except in counting them fortunate, for they had been grasped to the bosom of Allah as heroes and consigned to Paradise. But they have subsequently estimated that they suffered more than twice that number with an estimated 86,700 dead and countless wounded.

It might even be said that, in the end, the Anzacs gave as good as they got. Professor Geoffrey Blainey, one of our most noted historians, described it as an away draw. In the process of what turned out to be a military stalemate, more than half a million young warriors were wounded or died in a series of battles and endless skirmishes that never reached further inland than a man could walk at a brisk pace in half an hour from the pebbled beach where it had all begun.

The military objective on the first day had been to reach the third ridge and to have taken Hill 971, from which they would have been in a position to command the Narrows on the other side of the Peninsula and be able to attack the Turkish forts that protected this narrow strip of water. In this and everything else they had failed. It was obvious to the commanders on the ground that they could not have won and that they should have retreated from Turkish soil immediately. Hamilton, when advised, replied that he didn't have enough ships to move the troops off, and *'There is nothing for it but to dig yourselves right in and to stick it out.'*

The troops who survived the landing at Gallipoli were not to know that in their initial panic-driven advance in the hours immediately after dawn on the first day, they had reached the highest point they would attain until they returned after the surrender of Turkey in 1918 to bury their dead.

Someone had blundered terribly. And if, as was later maintained, the strong current had driven the pinnacles and the boats they towed a mile further north than they were supposed to be, then someone hadn't charted the tides or correctly judged the impact the current might play in the landing. Or if it was simply a case of the navy mistaking their position in the dark, either way, it was a fundamental mistake, an error of omission that was almost unthinkable and meant that strategically the landing at Gallipoli had failed.

There was only one man to blame, although in the context of the total war in Europe, the fiasco involving the landing at Gallipoli was seen by the British High Command as a relatively minor diversion. Slaughter in these proportions was often enough a daily occurrence in the killing fields of Flanders and the Somme, and Hamilton didn't even receive the mildest reproof. It was not until October 1915, when Hamilton's incompetence had become too manifest to be ignored any longer, that Lord Kitchener finally sacked him.

The casualties on the first day were never accurately known and were estimated at 4000 with 1700 wounded. As a further demonstration of Hamilton's incompetence, only two hospital ships had accompanied the attack and they had the capacity to treat only 700 wounded men. Furthermore, they would take no less than three days to reach Malta or Egypt and many of the wounded died on board of gangrene and other complications without ever having been attended to.

It has always been claimed that the first casualty of any war is the truth and it was no different at Gallipoli. Back home, the report released five days after the landing was that there had been minor casualties and that the Allies were sweeping the Turks away.

There is no better way to sum up the time the troops spent on this patch of ground than to quote a poet who was there. Sergeant Leon Gellert, of 10th Battalion, Gallipoli, January 1916, wrote these lyrics to a marching song:

There's a lonely stretch of hillocks:
There's a beach asleep and drear:
There's a battered broken fort beside the sea.
There are sunken, trampled graves:
And a little rotting pier:
And winding paths that wind unceasingly.

There's a torn and silent valley:
There's a tiny rivulet
With some blood upon the stones beside its mouth.
There are lines of buried bones:
There's an unpaid waiting debt:
There's a sound of gentle sobbing in the South.

CHAPTER 12

After Gallipoli

We disembarked at Mudros, the magnificent harbour of Lemnos, where I saw the S.S. *Mauritania*, 40,000 tons (or thereabouts), under steam about one hundred yards from the shore, such was the depth of the water in the harbour, which was an extinct volcano.

We spent Christmas Day on Lemnos, which was enjoyed by all, particularly as we received mail, including parcels that had been kept back pending our arrival from Gallipoli. I remember my joy at receiving a pipe and tin of Havelock tobacco in my parcel.

Lemnos was dull, but a haven after Gallipoli. We were given light duties, and only two incidents remain clear in my memory. Firstly, led by a Greek guide in sheepskin jacket and hat, we were taken over open and mountainous country to 'Thermos Springs' for a bath and a change of underwear.

We were all weak, and the climb and thinner atmosphere as we climbed higher brought about bouts of uncontrollable coughing. Literally hundreds of men collapsed, and those who kept going could look back down the mountainside for a mile or more at men lying on the ground, attended to by medical orderlies.

The springs were insignificant: a few trickles of luke-warm spa water from the rocks into basins carved out of the rock floor. The underclothing we had been issued felt as though it had been woven from barbed wire. It was, however, free of vermin. The march home was longer, but was along a made, olive-lined road through scenic country. We could never understand why we hadn't come that way.

The second incident of note was hilarious. The whole brigade (or it might have been the whole division) was lined up, twenty or thirty deep, for a review by, I think, the divisional commander – or it may have been by General Birdwood – when a hare broke cover from somewhere in front of us. No doubt confused, the hare made straight for the troops, and boots started to fly at it (it would have been a prize for the pot). Thousands of troops gave chase and, in the hurly-burly, knocked each other down. The hare miraculously escaped, ranks were re-formed, but the general had departed, probably in disgust.

Early in January we boarded a longish vessel, named *Minnewaska*, for Alexandria and, from there, proceeded by train to Tel el Kebir. We were greeted there by heavy rain, and no cover other than a few tarpaulins dumped on the sand. Our camp site was an old battleground where the British had defeated the Egyptians under Arabi Pasha in 1882. Just by kicking the sand, it was easy to find relics of those days in the form of rusted eating and cooking articles, spent bullets and bullet cases, and one day I unearthed the remains of an old Martini Henry rifle and bayonet.

This was the heyday of gambling, which was carried on nightly along about two miles of railway line that ran alongside the camp, the light being supplied by candles and improvised lamps fuelled by oil or fat. One man – he who had won our money from two pays on Gallipoli – was renowned to have won over six thousand pounds. He sent his money home, tried to follow it, and was picked up by military police in Ceylon, returned to England and sentenced to two years in Wandsworth Prison. The last time I saw him was in the outer at Flemington racecourse, with the backside out of his pants. I gave him ten shillings and he made a beeline to a bookmaker.

After about four weeks at Tel el Kebir we moved by train to Ismailia on the Suez Canal, and then by foot into the Sinai Peninsula about twelve miles from the Canal, where we started to dig trenches in sand many feet deep. As fast as we dug, the sand fell in until, having reached a depth of about five feet, the width at the top was about fifteen feet. We placed trusses made of bamboo and plaited rushes, trussed them top and bottom, and shovelled back the sand we had dug out. Then we lined the top with sandbags and fixed other trusses on top with openings to fire through at intervals, shovelled more sand on that as camouflage, and had very good trenches.

These trenches were to guard the canal should Johnny Turk again launch an attack against it. He was reported to be assembling troops at Beersheba, 120 miles away.

One incident is worth recording although it shows me as somewhat undisciplined. It was the habit to send out patrols of five men early in the morning. We would go out in diamond formation, with the N.C.O. in the centre, for about five miles and return shortly after break of day. The going was slow, except in the early stages where the sand was damp with the nightly heavy dew. Once the sun's rays appeared over the horizon, it would only take a short time for the sand to dry out, after which we'd sink ankle-deep with every step. The never-ending lines of sand dunes made things more difficult.

One morning we had gone over the five miles, which could only be guessed at, when the sergeant in the centre signalled that we should go back. Just at that moment, I spotted a figure in flowing robes on the top of the dune. He disappeared from sight, came up again, and so on with each succeeding dune. I tried to draw the sergeant's attention without success and then hailed the Arab – for such I guessed him to be. He looked my way but, beyond that, took no notice. I was in a quandary. It was believed that there were no Arabs between us and Beersheba, but we had orders not to shoot unless attacked – apparently by a Turkish patrol. I tried to catch up with the man – he was only about 300 yards distant – but he increased his speed and it soon became obvious that he was playing with me. By this time, my blood was up and, in the belief that it would halt him, I put a shot a couple of yards behind him. He disappeared in a flash and I didn't see him again.

The anger of the sergeant was nothing compared to that of the colonel who, mounted on his beautiful charger, Bobs, met us about a mile out from camp. The sound of the shot through the crisp still air of the early morning had been distinctively heard at the camp and the whole of the 2nd Division had been placed on 'stand to'. The colonel threatened a court martial, but he was a kindly man and I heard no more of it. My friends wondered at my forbearance in aiming to scare the Arab, but then, as a rule, the Australian troops did not like Arabs.

Despite the fact that we went without a wash during the five or six weeks we were in the desert, it was a healthy life. The sand was clean and we washed our eating and cooking utensils in it. The utensils had never been so clean, and never again were. Everything, including water, was brought to us by camels, long lines of them. They are unpleasant creatures and we soon learned to keep well clear of them.

In early March, we were relieved by the Otago Mounted Rifles. They were to arrive in the early morning and, on the appointed day, we struck camp at about four in the morning. The sun came up but there was no sign of our relief. The day wore on and we had to find what relief we could from the scorching sun under waterproof sheets, blankets, or whatever we had, stretched on top of rifles with their bayonets in the sand. About midday they arrived and we set off with somewhat diminished water bottles, laden with full equipment, a blanket, a greatcoat, rifle, ammunition, etc. on the long trek to Moascar on the Canal. About ten or eleven miles of it was over sand up to our ankles and the temperature was well over 100 °F. Water bottles ran dry and hundreds of men dropped along the route from heat exhaustion and lack of water, to be revived after water was brought to them and the cool air of the evening arrived.

Just before dusk we reached the water tanks on a made road, about a mile from the Canal. The tanks were rushed and the sympathetic Tommy guards made no effort to interfere.

A strange thing happened when we got onto the hard road. Relieved of the drag of the sand, each of our steps would come up about a foot above the road surface. We must have presented a strange sight, a body of several hundred heavily laden men high-stepping it along the road. About half a mile from Moascar we were met by a Scottish Pipe Band and the result was miraculous. Men who'd been in a comatose state and ready to drop from exhaustion straightened up and, having controlled our jerking knees, we marched into Moascar camp as though on parade.

The march was unanimously voted to be the worst the battalion had experienced.

CHAPTER 13

France

The Dardanelles Campaign left our small nation devastated. So many young lives were sacrificed for so little gained, or so it seemed to those at home by the middle of 1916. The daily delivery of telegrams from the War Office informing them of the death of a son or husband had become a familiar occurrence in every city suburb and country town. We were beginning to see the war through eyes very different from those which had watched the departure of the A.I.F. in 1914, when the fortunate lads chosen for the 'grand picnic in Europe' had sailed away.

In constructing the myth that is Gallipoli, it has become customary to blame the incompetence of the high-ranking British officers for the disaster of the Dardanelles

Campaign and equally to contrast this against the gallantry of the Australians and New Zealanders. It is as if, to a man, the officers were blundering fools and the men all tragic heroes. Of course this is not the case; not all British officers were inadequate to the task and as many Australian officers as their English counterparts made foolish decisions. For instance, it was an Australian, Colonel J. M Antill, who insisted that the third and fourth lines at The Nek sacrifice their lives when it was patently suicide to do so. As for the men, like any war, Gallipoli had its share of cowards and malingerers.

In terms of the entirety, the allies in Europe and Russia saw the fight against the Turks as a sideshow to the Western Front; the daily dead on the battlefields of Gallipoli and Suvla were small losses when compared to the slaughter that was taking place on the Russian Front and in Belgium and France. While the Anzacs had served their apprenticeship at Gallipoli with great distinction, it was now our turn to join our allies in the killing fields of Europe where, on one bad day at the Battle of the Somme, 18,000 men died. This easy disregard by the British High Command is best demonstrated by General Haig, who, while visiting Anzac Corps HQ, grew impatient with General Birdwood: *'You're not fighting Bashi-Bazouks now! This is a serious, scientific war!'* he shouted. The

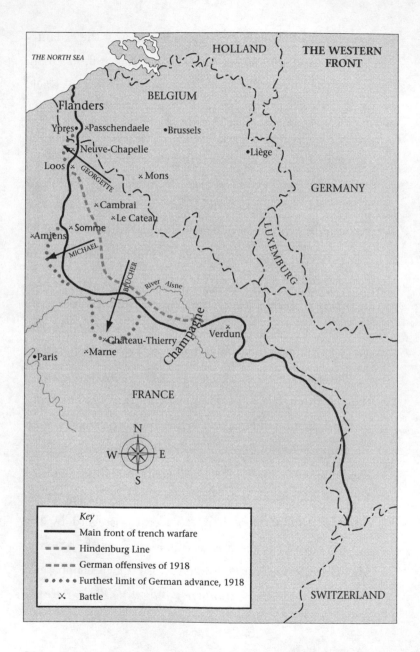

THE WESTERN
FRONT

Anzacs were soon to find out how different this war was to the one they'd recently fought and they were to do so beginning at Pozières and at Fromelles.

Any attempt to describe the war on the Western Front and at the same time to make sense of what was happening is going to be difficult, but there is a need to summarise what happened before the Anzacs arrived so that Roy Kyle's memoirs can be seen in some sort of context.

The war on the Western Front commenced in late 1914 with the Germans and the allies each dug in securely, the one waiting for the other to make the first real move in order to get things under way. Meanwhile, the real action was taking place on the Eastern Front, where the Germans were fighting the Russians.

In March 1915 Churchill began a blockade of German ports to weaken the German army, though with little success. The German navy, while not as big as the combined British and French, was nevertheless a formidable force and able to circumvent much of the blockade, which in the end proved unsuccessful. Churchill would eventually be sacked as Lord of the Admiralty for this and the misbegotten Dardanelles Campaign and would effectively play no further part in the policy direction of the war.

In the same month as the attempted blockade, the British took the initiative and attacked at Aubers, taking some ground and gaining great confidence from their efforts. In April the Germans retaliated and attacked Ypres, a mediaeval city in Flanders that was the key to the channel ports. Once again the British proved to be superior and the enemy were forced to withdraw, though in the process they bombarded this historical and ancient city to devastating effect.

It was a sign of things to come. Nothing was to be spared in the name of war where artillery now had the capacity to reduce cities of considerable size to rubble. Ypres was to be revisited three times, the last of these in July 1917 in a campaign lasting four months. In her book, *They Called It Passchendaele*, Lyn MacDonald wrote: *'Four years of war turned Ypres into a ghost town. Not a leaf grew on a tree, scarcely one stone stood upon another. From the battered ramparts the eye swept clean across a field of rubble to the swamplands beyond.'*

But this was 1915 and the first battle for control of Ypres, and the allies had every reason to feel they had the measure of the Germans on the Western Front. Confident of success, the British and the French launched another major attack in September, the British at Loos and the French at Champagne and Vimy Ridge.

At Loos the British outnumbered the Germans seven to one and believed they had the measure of the enemy but, instead, they were given a terrible drubbing. The defeat was eventually blamed on the fact that the British lacked artillery ammunition, but nonetheless the British lost 50,000 men and the Germans only half that number. By this time, the Western Front stretched from the channel ports to the Somme, a series of trenches stretching to the Swiss border.

In February 1916, it was the Germans' turn to mount a massive attack at Verdun, which was defended by the French. At first the French considered Verdun not strategically important, except that it was positioned at the start of the Champagne plain and was thus en route to Paris. The Germans opened the battle with nine hours of intensive shelling. Nothing as furious as this had hitherto taken place in the history of warfare. Still the French thought they were involved in no more than a tactical demonstration of enemy strength. How very wrong this proved to be. The Battle of Verdun was to rage for the remainder of the year and effectively petered out in December, by which time the French had suffered 337,231 casualties with 162,308 missing presumed dead, and the Germans an almost identical number, 337,000 with 100,000 missing presumed dead, a combined total of 714,231 casualties.

It was at Verdun that the allies began to realise that the Germans had prepared for a new kind of war and were much more innovative than the allies, who still carried into battle many of the notions of the past, including the by now quaint concept of the cavalry charge. The Germans were the first to use the modern machine gun in vast numbers. It will be recalled that it was the German machine gun that became the most destructive weapon at Gallipoli and for which the Anzacs had no answer. The Germans had also invented the flame thrower and developed telescopic sights superior to anything the allies possessed. Moreover, they had organised their fledgling airforce into a reasonably sophisticated reconnaissance and sometime bombing unit to a much greater extent than the allies.

The allies caught up, though, and even exceeded the German capability to innovate, in particular with a superior artillery and the introduction of a light magazine-fed machine gun to match that of the Germans. Towards the end, they also created the Royal Flying Corps and the Royal Naval Air Service, turning both into effective airstrike units.

Australia created the Australian Flying Corps in 1917, and there was an immediate rush to join it. Among these would-be gallant young men in their flying machines was a disgruntled private who'd had his fill of mud and slush and the dangerous business of the Flying Pig mortar bomb, one Roy Kyle.

One fortunate pilot, presumably in the Royal Flying Corps, in a letter home in 1918 described the pilot's life: *'Wheeling and circling like a flock of hawks, firing on the enemy, then returning to a bath, a good meal and the gramophone playing. Knock spots off the infantry, doesn't it?'*

It should be pointed out that the attrition rate of pilots was as high proportionately as that of the men in the trenches. It was only that there were a lot fewer of them. Roy's application to be a pilot in one of the two Australian aircraft, like several thousand others, was rejected.

Verdun was to set the pattern for the war to come. In nine months of fighting, the lines were much as they had been in February. In an attempt to break this stalemate, the British decided to launch an attack of their own to force the Germans to fight on two fronts and, by so doing, relieve the French. This was to become known as the Battle of the Somme and it was here that the European war begins for the Anzacs.

The British believed that they would need more troops and summoned the Australian 1st and 2nd Divisions and the New Zealand Division, together known as 1st Anzac Corps, from Egypt, with the Australian 4th Division joining them from England.

The battle began on 1 July 1916 as a planned offensive on a front twenty-three miles long, and commenced by the

British shelling the German defences for eight days. The Germans had built a network of almost impregnable bunkers, many of them of deep concrete construction, and the shelling did little to harm them or to prevent their ability to fight. Seven hundred and fifty thousand men, eighty per cent from the British Expeditionary Force, with the remainder French, entered the battle. In all, twenty-seven allied divisions came up against sixteen German, the numerical odds greatly in favour of the allies. The Anzacs were still on their way from Egypt when the first onslaught against the enemy occurred. On their first day of fighting, the British took appalling losses against the enemy machine guns, with 58,000 casualties and 18,000 dead.

As had happened at Verdun, the ensuing months and years at the Somme became a stalemate. It was a battlefield consisting of many smaller battles as each side fought to gain the advantage. In July the newly arrived Australian 1st, 2nd and 4th plus the New Zealanders, a force consisting of 40,000 Australians and 18,500 New Zealanders, marched down from near Armentières and took part in the attack on Pozières Ridge. The 5th Division, the first of the Australian divisions to arrive in France, had already seen battle at Fromelles and so nearly all of the Australian forces were now involved in the European sector of the war.

As the Australians marched into battle, the British expressed the fear that the Anzacs, new to this type of battle, would be undertrained and not up to the task. Nevertheless, the Australians and the New Zealanders acquitted themselves well and showed that they could endure the heat of battle as well, if not better than, most. It was in the Pozières sector that Private Roy Kyle entered the war in Europe.

The Somme would prove to be very different from the conditions in Turkey and it was where the Anzacs were first issued with steel helmets, which had not been used at Gallipoli. They also came up against trench mortars and were made aware of the concept of a gas attack. It was not only the new equipment they found strange but they also had to constantly prepare and maintain the trenches destroyed by the German heavy artillery at Pozières. In the hard earth at Gallipoli, the trenches, once dug, stayed dug and seldom needed major repairs. By comparison with the mud and dampness of the Somme, those trenches were magnificent structures, some of which still remain in position today. By contrast, the winter of 1916–17 was unusually wet and cold and the trenches soon turned to mud and slime. Sandbags made up much of the walls of the communication trenches, as anything dug with any depth became waterlogged.

In Gallipoli, the natural disasters had been bugs, lice, flies and rats. Here at the Somme they were much the same – bugs, lice and rats – but added to these were trench foot, from the eternal mud and slush, and trench fever, the latter accounting for a huge number of casualties. Kyle himself was hospitalised with trench fever, first in an American hospital in France and later in England. Trench fever, carried by body lice, was caused by highly infectious bacteria that bred best in overcrowded and unsanitary conditions. The symptoms were a loss of energy, severe pain in the muscles and bones, headache, weight loss and severe skin rash, and the illness was characterised by repeated cycles of fever. Trench foot, on the other hand, proved almost as vexatious and was caused by standing for hours, even days, in mud and water without being able to dry one's feet or change one's socks. In addition, the puttees wound tightly around legs restricted circulation and compounded the problem. Feet swelled as the condition attacked the ball of the foot, making it almost impossible to remove one's boots. Soon after, the foot would go black and, if left untreated, the toes and even, in extreme cases, the entire foot would need to be amputated. The condition was also extremely painful.

Sickness was almost inevitable. The European winter of 1916–17 was claimed to be the harshest in forty years.

In heartbreaking mud and slush and extreme cold, it became difficult to get supplies to the trenches and water and food became scarce. The men would often be forced to drink water boiled down from snow contaminated by dead bodies.

Jim McPhee, a serviceman who had endured the severe European winters, speaking to Patsy Adam-Smith in *The Anzacs*, summed up the various diseases and natural afflictions suffered by the men in the trenches: *'Our bodies – some hobbled with trench feet, some had toes off with frostbite; some shook with trench fever – a sort of rheumatic fever that weakened the bones and joints; many had sores that wouldn't heal, all had lice; many had running noses and eyes long after they'd come back from treatment, from being gassed, and almost all had experienced shell shock to some degree – the slightest being the shakes, or bleeding from the ears, ranging to complete dementia.'*

While rats were common enough at Gallipoli, here they were everywhere. In fact, it became a sport to smoke them out of holes and then to pick them off with rifles and bayonets. Suzanne Welborn, in her book *Lords of Death*, quotes an Australian soldier: *'It really is good sport. Rats abound in thousands and are loathed if only because they feed on the corpses lying about. They are too surfeited very often to run.'*

Today we refer to gas and other invasive agents as

'weapons of mass destruction', as if they are new to war. We often forget that chemical warfare was introduced in the Great War and, while missing in World War II and the Korean War, it was reintroduced as napalm and Agent Orange in Vietnam by the Americans, and with devastating effect as sarin gas by Saddam Hussein against the Kurds in northern Iraq.

On 22 April 1915 in Ypres, salient chemical warfare was used for the first time when the Germans opened 6000 cylinders of chlorine gas along a five-mile front. Chlorine is a lung irritant, and allied soldiers breathing it in for the first time abandoned their trenches and fled panic-stricken. Many of them died a slow, agonising death by suffocation, some of which was aided by the added pulmonary constriction caused by panic. So great was this panic that it left a three-mile gap in the allied defences. The Germans, unaware of the success of their ghastly experiment, failed to capitalise on the havoc they'd caused. The men would later learn to use a rag soaked with urine clutched to their mouth and nose, as the ammonia in the urine neutralised the chlorine gas.

There was an immediate outcry that the Germans had abandoned the last vestiges of decency and had descended to the level of animals. Nevertheless, the allies were quick to retaliate and by the end of 1915 they, too, were using chlorine gas, by which time the Germans had added phosgene, an even more powerful suffocating gas, to their chemical arsenal.

The Australians were to experience both of these chemicals in a comparatively minor degree but in 1917 the Germans turned to mustard gas, an infinitely more lethal mixture and so painful that most sufferers were strapped to their beds lest they tried to take their own lives. Death often took up to five weeks.

In fact, gas was the great horror both sides feared almost above anything else. It could come on the evening breeze, silent, invisible and deadly. It could reach you when you fell into an exhausted sleep and you'd never wake up. Or you'd wake up choking, vomiting or coughing up blood, with the smell of pineapple and pepper (chlorine) or rotten fish (phosgene) in your nostrils when it was too late to reach for your mask. If it was mustard gas, it was odourless and therefore even more sinister and deadly. With a change of wind, the gas intended for the Hun could turn back and invade your own trenches and, although far more men died by means of conventional weapons, nothing instilled more fear in a soldier's heart. The Germans had sown the wind but they were to reap the whirlwind. Towards the end of the war, the allies were using artillery-delivered mustard gas to a far greater extent than the enemy.

Major Donald Coutts of the 6th Field Ambulance wrote: *'Another gas bombardment . . . there were 200 gassed men . . . many of them were vomiting and coughing. I evacuated most of them. We sent them off in parties of 5 and 6 – walking behind the other, with their hands on the shoulder of the man in front, and a stretcher bearer leading the way. Many of them could not see at all.'*

Wilfred Owen, the war poet, put it even more starkly: *'the blood . . . gurgling from froth-corrupted lungs.'*

The urine-soaked rag was soon replaced by a cloth gas helmet, which provided somewhat better protection, and around the time the Anzacs arrived it, too, had been replaced by a cumbersome, thoroughly uncomfortable but nevertheless effective box respirator with a breathing tube attached to a canister. In the official history of the 24th Battalion A.I.F., this description of the respirator is given: *'The small gas respirators . . . were little more than suffocating masks . . . Many a man had his face well blistered, though no gas came near him. Yet we cherished these crude masks as a miser clings to gold. We knew that at any moment they might be all that stood between us and death.'*

At first, the fighting at the Somme was not as sporadically fierce as Gallipoli in terms of man-to-man combat. It was more sophisticated and the conditions in the trenches, despite the tendency they had to collapse in the wet weather, were a distinct improvement from the months on Turkish soil. Here also the troops were frequently allowed behind the lines where they could relax – something almost unknown in Gallipoli. C. E. W. Bean, the official A.I.F. historian, wrote: *'Here [trench warfare] was less tense and more comfortable. Food . . . was more varied, water [that ever scarce commodity at Gallipoli] was "laid on" through pipes . . . here were communication trenches, winding through green fields and hedgerows . . . There were shops in the villages, and estaminets [country cafès], selling Flemish beer and cheap wine . . . further back were excellent British canteens, reading and writing rooms. Army baths where underclothing was periodically freed from fleas and lice.'*

In those early weeks in Europe, the veterans from Gallipoli thought themselves damned near in paradise. In May 1916, Captain Biddle of the 4th Battery wrote home: *'We are still having a picnic as far as fighting goes. We have been a month in action but have done very little shooting. We are now going into a rest. Some war this one! It's a bit of a change from Gallipoli isn't it?'*

This rest behind the lines very often meant that the soldiers were billeted in some French villager's cowshed, where the easygoing way and ability of Australians to adapt to the social conditions of the village meant that they were soon taking up quarters with the family as a welcome boarder. Many of the subsequent friendships lasted, via correspondence, throughout the lives of the diggers. Roy Kyle speaks fondly of being billeted with a French lady while at signalling school.

The Australians were soon to learn that the Germans were more skilful than the Turks and the war potentially more dangerous because of elements outside the control of soldiers, who had been taught to fight with courage armed only with rifle, bayonet and hand-thrown, home-made bombs. The courage of men like Simpson and his donkey and the one-man war of Lance-Corporal Jacka V.C., who, singlehanded, charged a Turkish trench and killed nine Turks, had little or no place here. The romantic notion of war, where one warrior faced another in equal contest, had disappeared forever. Gas had come silently to stay, aeroplanes growled in the sky overhead and dropped bombs right on top of you, artillery was infinitely more accurate, larger and more deadly, and the trench mortars seemed to know exactly where you were. Courage, daring and initiative, characteristics of the Anzac soldier, had become a less important factor in the winning of battles.

Nonetheless, the Anzacs were happy to be at last fighting the Germans. Germany had been the original and major foe and, for all the genuine respect the Australians had gained for the Turk, they thought of the Hun, Fritz or Jerry, as the more worthy of the two adversaries.

To understand the Western Front is to realise that it was waged mostly as a stationary state of siege, with the trench the home base, or the status quo, broken by large-scale assaults and much smaller raids. The major attacks were well-prepared events and, unlike the smaller raids, no surprise was possible. The artillery would pound the German trenches to soften them up and to force them to take cover, at the same time alerting them to the coming battle. If the Germans could withstand the initial bombardment, they had merely to wait for the allies to come across No Man's Land and up against their own barbed wire to respond to the attack with their machine guns, rifles and mortar shells. Any rapid progress was inevitably halted at the wire where men had to cut or crawl or even worm their way through to finally leap into the enemy trenches. In fact, those involved in such an assault were always anxious to get into the comparative safety of the German trenches. Even in the often pitched battles that ensued, the odds of surviving the hand-to-hand fighting were somewhat better than being caught in the open.

Fighting within the trenches was chaotic. With whole sections of the German front-line trenches wrecked by preceding British artillery, progress was difficult and dangerous.

Men became lost in the maze of ditches and tunnels, where behind every twist or turn the enemy might be lurking. It was in these assaults that the Australians began to earn a name for themselves by climbing back out of the trenches they were raiding to run along the edge hurling Mills bombs down at the enemy they could now clearly see from above. This meant they exposed themselves to sniper fire and greatly increased their chances of being killed. Although some diggers seemed to relish this dance with death, and the Germans made mention of the fact that they greatly feared the Australians because of it, major assaults of this nature seldom proved decisive and caused a great many deaths, usually without changing the status quo. It would sometimes appear to the men in the trenches that the generals were playing a game, a type of chess where the outcome was never clear, in the happily accepted knowledge that it would be a lengthy contest with the need to sacrifice a great many pieces.

Trench raids were somewhat different in nature, there was no artillery barrage to warn the enemy and the element of surprise was an essential ingredient. Crossing No Man's Land and cutting the German wire was done silently by a small raiding party. Riflemen would fan out in the lead, followed by bombers carrying Mills bombs and, at the rear, two Lewis guns, their job to prevent a counterattack. Some of the men carried trench clubs, homemade affairs weighted with lead or studded with metal that, as in the close confines of the trenches, often proved more useful and just as deadly as a bayoneted rifle.

The fighting during a raid was always fierce, with no holds barred, and was usually over in fifteen minutes. Seriously wounded men had to be left behind as the return journey, with the Germans now alerted, was always more dangerous and a raiding party simply couldn't be encumbered by a wounded man who couldn't fend for himself in the recrossing of No Man's Land.

The intention of these raids had little to do with the large-scale outcomes; they were often enough mounted to capture prisoners for interrogation, four or five Germans together with an officer, who, it was thought, possessed more information than the men. Capturing one man was not enough, he would be especially targeted by his own machine-gun fire to make sure he didn't reach the allied trenches alive. When this happened, it meant the entire raid had been wasted.

The Somme also involved pitched battles on a large scale at terrible cost to both sides. This is best illustrated by Lieutenant John Raws, a journalist before the war, when writing to a friend: *'The glories of the Great Push are great, but the horrors are greater. With all I'd heard by word of mouth, with all I had imagined in my mind, I yet never conceived that war could be so dreadful. The carnage in our little sector was as bad, or worse, than that of Verdun, and yet I never saw a body buried in ten days. And when I came on the scene the whole place, trenches and all was spread with dead. We had neither time nor space for burial, the wounded could not be got away. They stayed with us and died, pitifully, with us, and they rotted. The stench of the battlefield spread for miles around. And the sight of the limbs, the mangled bodies and the stray heads . . . Do you know that I saw with my own eyes a score of men go raving mad.'*

In another letter Lieutenant Raws, this time to his brother, also a lieutenant, wrote: *'We do all our fighting and moving at night, and the confusion of pushing through a barrage of enemy shell in the dark is pretty appalling . . . I have kept my nerve so far . . . the bravest of all often lose it, courage does not count here . . . we are lousy, stinking, ragged, unshaven, sleepless. My tunic is rotten with other men's blood and partly splattered with a comrades brains.'* Lieutenant Raws was killed on 16 August 1916.

Before Roy Kyle arrived with his division from Egypt, the 5th Division, already in France, was to be a major participant in the battle for Fromelles, a village near Armentières. The aim of the operation was to seize German positions at a salient known as 'Sugar Loaf'. It was thought at the time this would prevent the Germans from sending reinforcements down from Belgium to the Somme.

It was the landing at Gallipoli all over again. The result was a complete fiasco and proved to be one of the most misconceived operations mounted by the British on the Western Front. Brigadier H. E. 'Pompey' Elliott, the popular Australian general at Gallipoli and not the senior general responsible for the planning of this operation, stood weeping as he shook the hands of the Australian survivors as they made their way back from the German lines. In one night the A.I.F. suffered 5533 casualties, and the trench floors were cluttered with the dead and the wounded.

Corporal H. H. Harris, later describing it in *The Broken Years*, said, *'It was like a butcher's shop. They lay in heaps behind the parapets . . . Chaos and weird noises like thousands of iron foundries, deafening and dreadful, coupled with the roar of high explosives.'*

W. H. Downing (in his book *To the Last Ride*) wrote: *'Sheaves and streams of bullets swept like whirling knives. There were many corpses hung inert on our wire, there were many corpses hung inert on their wire, but [we] . . . surged forward.*

'There was the frightful chaos of minenwerfers (German

trench mortars) shaking the ground into waves, trailing lines
of sparks criss-crossed in the gloom, swerving just before they
fell, confounding, dreadful, abhorred far more than shells,
killing by their very concussion . . .'

Mortars used at both Fromelles and Pozières were a
new experience to the Australians and one they soon grew
to dislike intensely. Here was a weapon almost anyone
could use. Once it found your range, it could drop down
with accuracy, intensity and persistence to create havoc
within a trench. A great deal of effort would go into trying
to locate and destroy this highly effective weapon, not an
easy task since the basic trench mortar was light and easily
moved from place to place. Roy Kyle, like the remarkable
Scurry of the self-firing rifle fame, found himself being
trained in trench mortars where, apart from a short stint
digging trenches, he was to spend the greater part of his
time on the Western Front.

The simplest trench mortar required very little training to use and was operated by the infantry themselves.
It consisted of three parts: a base plate, a barrel and a
bipod for supporting the barrel. A bomb was dropped
down the tube and its impact ignited a propellant to fire
the shell, which exploded upon landing. Unlike conventional artillery, which observed the age-old principle of a
cannon, the mortar shell travelled in a high arc to land

on top of the target. The pictures one often sees of the WWI battlefield with thousands of potholes are the work of mortar explosions, the unsightly acne on the face of the battlefield.

However, Roy Kyle was not to be granted the good fortune of a lightweight trench mortar but became, instead, a member of the 'Suicide Club'. That is to say, he was a member of the Trench Mortar Service, men who operated heavy mortars which had to stay put in the one place and so could easily be located by the enemy and quickly terminated. The volunteers for this particular service were not given great odds in the survival stakes and thus earned their nickname.

Of all the available British mortars, the 'Flying Pig' was the largest and got its name simply because it was about the size of the average French farmyard pig purchased from the local farmers by the catering sergeant for the officers' mess. It needed to be solidly based and, once set in position, could not be moved without a great deal of effort to dislodge it from the mud and slush of battlefield conditions.

With the disaster at Fromelles involving the 5th Division over, the Australians in the 1st, 2nd and 4th Divisions were brought into the battle at Pozières in July and August. It was here that Roy Kyle's battery was to bring their Flying

Pigs. He reports that, due to the ground being so heavily churned up by German artillery, they couldn't get these heavy mortars sufficiently grounded to fire accurately and so they didn't play the significant role at Pozières that was expected of them.

The village of Pozières was to be the only allied victory at this point in the Battle of the Somme and this was largely due to the courage of the Australians. The British had already made five unsuccessful attempts to take the village, whereas the Anzacs took it without too much difficulty, with the Germans retreating to the ridge behind the village, which they then continued to hold. The Germans counterattacked on four separate occasions in an attempt to recapture the village but were beaten back by the diggers on every occasion.

By taking the village, the allies had achieved their objective, which was to open the road to Bapaume, and there was no need at the time to take the ridge. Besides, the Germans held the high ground, and any further advance would likely to be met with devastating artillery fire so that it was foolish to attack their positions. The Germans confirmed this when they pounded the village and the battleground until it was reduced to rubble and the ground became a desert of brown, crater-pocked earth without a single tree or hedgerow left standing.

However, General Sir Hubert Gough, the commander of the British Reserve Army, who outranked the Australian generals, ignored the generals' appeals for commonsense and insisted the Australians push on to attempt to take the Pozières ridge. The Germans couldn't believe their luck and hit them with everything they had in the most serious bombardment Australian troops would endure during the entire war. In less than seven weeks, the Australians lost 23,000 men, killed, wounded or missing. Pozières once again confirmed the distrust the Anzacs held for the British High Command. They ever afterwards reckoned that in both battles, Fromelles and Pozières, a great many of their mates had been needlessly slaughtered and that they'd been thoroughly dudded by the British High Command.

The war journalist, later to become England's poet laureate, John Masefield, described the battlefield around Pozières as: *'more densely sown with Australian sacrifice than any other place on earth.'* And one survivor of the battle, Captain N. M. Cuthbert said, *'Our trenches were very shallow in parts and full of our and enemy dead on which the swarms of black flies and maggots – trenches reeking and crawling.'*

In what must seem a strange paradox, life on the Somme, so synonymous with death and destruction, was, in the times between battles and raids, very boring. It was on such occasions that the Australian love of sport came to the fore in the ranks. To relieve the tedium, a game of cricket or football, usually Australian Rules or Rugby Union, though sometimes the code more often played by the British which featured a round ball, was common, with fierce rivalry between different units. These games would often take place within the enemy's artillery range.

There is a story told, usually on occasions such as Anzac Day and almost certainly apocryphal, of a scratch game of cricket taking place on a patch of ground situated only just behind the lines when a mortar shell landed precisely on the batting crease, instantly killing the batsman. Up went the umpire's finger: 'You're out, lad, and so are we,' he shouted. 'Run like hell, boys!'

The next three major offences for our troops occurred in 1917 with the first of these against the Hindenburg Line at Bullecourt in April and May with 10,000 casualties. The second was at Messines in June, which was the 3rd Division's first significant action.

Of all the allied attacks, the Messines ridge was probably the most meticulously planned. In the two years preceding the attack, nineteen huge tunnels were dug beneath the German positions under the ridge and filled with 50–70,000 pounds of explosives. On 7 June the attack took place, with the underground tunnel explosions completely taking the Germans by surprise. The explosion was said to be heard in London.

Over the next few days the Germans, completely demoralised by the biggest explosion in the history of warfare, were pushed back relentlessly with the allies over-running all their trenches, taking Messines' heights and gaining around 2000 yards.

The victory was so conclusive that it prompted King George V to pay a visit to the troops to congratulate them. Nevertheless, the cost was high with 26,000 casualties over the five days of fighting, including 7000 Australians and 5000 New Zealanders.

As the months and years dragged on, the Anzacs became thoroughly seasoned veterans who had long since come to terms with the prospect of their own death. Many were sick and all were intensely weary and disillusioned, yet they knew that they were required to fight on and they bolstered their courage with the thought that *it's twice as bad for Jerry shittin' himself across the ridge ahead, him knowing the Diggers are comin' to get him.*

Many of the men began to suffer from shell shock, a problem previously unheard of, as no one had seen anything like the scale of sustained shelling, bombing and artillery fire these men were now forced to endure. At first the symptoms were put down to malingering and cowardice, but as some of the men shot themselves while others simply went mad, the military began to realise they were confronting a problem of significant proportions.

One veteran, Archie Barwick, tells in Gammage's *The Broken Years* of the effects of shell shock in a trench he was in: *'Men were driven stark, staring mad and more than one of them would rush out of the trench over towards the Germans. Any amount of them could be seen crying and sobbing like children their nerves completely gone.'*

The next involvement of the Australian divisions took place across an eight-mile front at Ypres on 7 October 1917. This was the third occasion that the mediaeval city was involved in an attempt to push the Germans back from the Belgian coast and, of the three battles, this one proved the most intense, with horrendous casualties on both sides.

Haig, the British general commanding the battle, decided to risk everything in an attempt to land a knock-out blow and capture the German-controlled village of Passchendaele on the heights above Ypres. Even in terms of the poor leadership not untypical of the times, it was a foolish decision and involved the Australians in some of the fiercest fighting of the war. Despite the odds being stacked against them, the Anzac Corps had three spectacular victories: taking Menin Road Ridge, Polygon Wood and Broodseinde Ridge.

Finally, exhausted, the Anzacs were withdrawn and the Canadian Corps were handed the job of trying to capture the village. They attacked five times with great courage to eventually take the position from the Germans. The eight-week campaign had cost the British 400,000 men, the Germans a similar amount, the Anzacs 38,000 men.

Lloyd George, when prime minister of England, would say at the conclusion of the war, *'Third Ypres, with the Somme and Verdun, will always rank as the most gigantic, tenacious, grim, futile and bloody fights ever waged in the history of war.'*

General Monash, who would command the Anzacs and the Canadians in the final assault against the Germans, was appalled by the way his countrymen were used in the third Ypres battle, in particular at Bullecourt and Passchendaele. *'It is bad to cultivate the habit of criticism of higher authority, and I do so with hesitation . . . Our men are being put into the hottest fighting and are being sacrificed in harebrained ventures, like Bullecourt and Passchendaele, and there is no one in the War Cabinet to lift a voice in protest.'*

Despite the terrible losses at Ypres, the Anzacs, buoyed by their success, were still keen to fight. Their spirits were surprisingly high at the thought that the fortunes of war were turning in their favour and that victory was now distinctly possible. They wanted to be there at the finish and were reluctant to be pulled out of the line in early 1918 and so miss being involved in the opening stages of the massive German offensive. The Germans, conscious that the Americans were about to enter the war, knew that it was basically now or never. With the strength of the Yanks against them, they couldn't hope to win. This was to be their last all-out attempt at victory over the allies. It was on for one and all and the Australians wanted to be in at the beginning of the stoush.

In April 1918, with the Australian units well rested over the winter, they returned with great enthusiasm to the fray. Roy Kyle recalls, *'An exhilarating period as, for the first time, we felt we were really winning.'* They fought with a toughness that became legendary among the French and helped to blunt the tremendous German offensive and then went on the offensive themselves.

Then came the best news they'd had all war. On 31 May 1918, John Monash, the son of Polish–Jewish immigrants, was promoted to Lieutenant General and made the Australian Corps commander. It was an appointment accepted with huge enthusiasm by the Anzacs. They had fought with Monash in Gallipoli and appreciated his attitude towards his troops. They knew him to be a miser with the lives of the men under his command and they appreciated that he was a master in the art of tactical planning.

Now, in this final onslaught against the Germans, Monash applied careful planning, using what he termed 'controlled aggression', brought about by the employment of intelligent use of tanks, aeroplanes and infantry. Above all, he was Australian and didn't think himself above his men, so he informed them quite openly of his plan of attack. Every man, down to the lowliest rifleman under his command, had some idea of the planned outcome and, for the first time, fought with this singular purpose and responsibility in mind.

The result was hugely gratifying. The Australians fighting with the Canadians and a part of Rawlinsons Fourth British Army commanded by Monash took 30,000 German prisoners and gained territory deep into the German front. The Battle of Amiens in August, known as the 'Black Day', proved one of the decisive breakthroughs in the war when the allies finally breached the Hindenburg Line. It was here that the Australians and the Canadians played a truly major role, though not without enormous cost, the A.I.F. sustaining 21,000 casualties.

On 5 October, much to the chagrin of the men who wanted to carry on in what they believed would soon be a victory against the Germans, they were withdrawn from the battle. They were to be given a short rest with the promise that they would come back into action early in the new year.

This was never to happen. Germany surrendered and signed the armistice on 11 November, and the promise of 'home just after Christmas' was finally fulfilled, four years after the *Sydney Morning Herald* had promised. In those four years, 58,961 young Australians had died. Another 166,811 men had been wounded, 87,865 were sick, and many of them would be semi-invalids for the remainder of their lives. It had been an enormous price to pay.

And so the war to end all wars came to an end. We had given of our best and covered ourselves in glory, but in so doing sacrificed our young men. We suffered the highest casualty rate of any of the national armies who'd fought in the war. To this dubious distinction was added yet another unique fact, ours was the only army on either side to go to war as volunteers.

———◈———

We were at Moascar for a few days and on 21 March embarked on the S.S. *Lake Michigan* bound for Marseilles, where we disembarked and entrained for the front area. We were two or three days on the train, on harsh third-class seats, six to a carriage, and took turns to sleep on the seats, the floor and the luggage racks. The tedium of the journey was relieved by the lovely country we passed through. We hadn't seen really green fields since leaving Australia and here we passed through unending miles of them; a lovely green, lighter than the green of our own country – it got darker as we went further north, with white farmhouses and, every now and again, a white chateau on a hill. For some reason unknown to us, we stopped at Lyon for about an hour at the end of a high bridge over the Rhone, where we had our first view of the French girls, who came out of shops in the street below the high railway line where we were imprisoned. They were soon engulfed by a swarm of children to whom we threw coins. We skirted Paris – saw the top of the Eiffel Tower – and detrained at Aire, from where we moved to Robecq and were billeted in cow sheds.

Robecq appeared to be an uninteresting village, but we saw little of it as, for most of the time there, we were quarantined because of an outbreak of some disease or other. Number 12 platoon was not affected by it, which is probably the reason I have forgotten what it was – possibly measles.

We were bored and one evening Jack Maugham, with whom I had became friendly at Gallipoli, and I went AWL for a few hours and visited the village of Erquinghem a few miles away. It was little, if any, better than Robecq but we discovered the sweet taste of malaga, and drank too much of it.

A week or ten days at Robecq and we moved to Fleurbaix in the Armentières sector, only about three miles from the front line. It had been shelled considerably but not completely destroyed, and there were a number of buildings standing. It was a quiet sector, but our artillery soon altered that. Number 12 platoon was billeted in the deserted school and we slept on tables, the floor, or anywhere we could find enough room to stretch out. It was almost a relief to go into the line, where the main excitement was in destroying rats.

The environment, however, was wonderful compared to Gallipoli. About a hundred yards from the school was the local *estaminet* where we could sit and drink beer and wines and eat fried eggs, all served by Yvette and Marie, to whom we nightly offered our hearts to no avail.

One memorable event was when a gas alarm went off. We fell in, donned masks and, in anticipation of an attack, marched up long saps to the front line, but nothing happened. Poor fastidious Maugham, having imbibed too freely of *vin rouge*, was sick in his gas mask.

About the end of March or early April, we moved a few miles to L'Halle-o-Beau, where we worked nightly like navvies digging deep trenches to lay cables for the artillery. Most nights it rained and the ground was a quagmire. The odd shell and the whine of bullets speeded up the work as the deeper we dug the safer we were. We spent so much time on this work that the battalion became known as 'The Mud Slingers', a sobriquet which was short-lived.

It was here that my membership of the 24th Battalion effectively ended. About a fortnight after moving to L'Halle-o-Beau, I was ordered by the Regimental Sergeant-Major to spruce myself up and to report to Divisional Headquarters for guard duty. On arrival at H.Q. I found several others, from various battalions of the 2nd Division waiting in an ante-room and learned that I was a member of the newly formed section of Divisional Guides. Our job was to learn all emergency roads leading to the front at Fromelles, where Australian troops – 5th Division – were soon to suffer over 5000 casualties in fifteen and a half hours in a hopeless attack that was launched with the objective of preventing the transfer of German troops to the Somme, where the first great battle in that area was soon to commence.

We were based on Bac St Maur, and for about four weeks left entirely to our own devices. Someone at Divisional H.Q. then remembered us and decided we were 'surplus to requirement' – in other words, 'not required' – and we were ordered to report back to our various units. We had learnt our 'roads', which were only lines on maps and ran through grasslands and crops to the reserve trenches.

While at Bac St Maur, we were billeted at the local *estaminet* and Madame, for ten francs per week from each of us, prepared meals from our rations, adding her own potatoes, and served them on a table with a clean white tablecloth. We slept upstairs on palliasses in a large dormitory-like room.

Two events which occurred at Bac St Maur are worth recording. The first relates to a Confirmation dinner for Jeanne (who had been confirmed at seven that morning), the youngest member of Madame's family, which, quite by accident, I attended. The morning, I remember, was lovely and sunny. I felt unwell and, as there was little to do at the time, the sergeant in charge of the group excused me and I returned to the billet to find great excitement in the preparation of an elaborate feast. I went upstairs, hoping to sleep but there was too much noise below. Two or three hours later the elder sister, Germaine, a fat and jolly girl of sixteen or seventeen, came up demanding that I join the party.

Reluctantly, I did so, to find about thirty aunts, uncles, cousins, etc., etc., all done up in their stiff Sunday-go-to-meeting clothes, had arrived from various parts of northern France. I had never seen so many French people in one bunch. The women were busy setting a long trestle table and the men were busy pouring *vin rouge* into themselves, and proceeded to pour it into me with the result that my squeamishness soon disappeared. They must have all contributed food, for the table was laden with it. The dinner was hilarious; never had I enjoyed a meal so much. There were numerous toasts, all of course in French, of which I understood but little. After the dinner the men repaired to the skittle alley at the side of the building, to play skittles for a sou a time. Skittles is the poor relation of the modern game of ten-pin bowling and on this occasion was played on the bare ground. After each game the losers bought more red wine, and each subsequent game became more hilarious, and the 'oohs and ahs' accompanied by roars of laughter came thick and fast. It was all in good spirit and there were no arguments. I got away, somewhat unsteadily, when the others in the group came in at about five, but the celebrations carried on into the night, and the guests were a sorry lot as they straggled off to their various destinations the following morning. I had a very sore head.

A few days after the Confirmation dinner, on a bright balmy night, the second incident occurred, in which Jeanne, seven years old, was again the central figure. At about eleven the terrifying screech of the village gas alarm sounded and Jeanne appeared at the top of the stairs calling 'Jack! Jack!', the name which had been bestowed on me when I first entered camp at Seymour, mainly, I think, because there was at that time a prominent Victorian fast bowler by the name of Jack Kyle, and which I had never bothered to correct, preferring it to 'Roy'. On my answering her, she came straight to my bunk and without a word got under the blanket and clung to me, obviously in great fear. She was soon followed by a shocked mother (Madame) who demanded that she surface and come down to her own bed immediately. The more Madame ordered and the more I pleaded, the tighter she clung. In a mixture of broken French and English, having assured Madame that Jeanne would be quite safe, she retired, presumably to her own bed. Jeanne slept peacefully throughout the night, but being fearful of waking her should I move, I did not close an eye. I think the little girl instinctively turned to me, because on several occasions I had played hopscotch and catchy in the backyard with her after returning later in the afternoon from the day's work. It left a wonderful memory . . .

I found the battalion at Bois Grenier, a few miles from L'Halle-o-Beau, where they had finished their cable-laying. After a few weeks away it felt like joining a new unit. There was a lot of talk about a new machine-gun company to be formed, but nothing definite. There was, however, a few days after rejoining, a call for volunteers for a heavy trench mortar unit being formed. It was to be attached to the artillery and was to be equipped with large trench mortars which fired a bomb or shell known as the 'Flying Pig'. After much thought I decided to join. In announcing my intention, I was implored by my friends not to on the grounds that it would be joining a suicide club. My mind was made up, much as I disliked leaving the friends I had made. After a year in the infantry I was satisfied that not only did it take the brunt of the fighting, but it was also the workhorse of the army. Only on those rare occasions when they were taken for a spell well back from the front line was there any let up for them anywhere within several miles of the line, and their nights would be occupied in carrying all sorts of materials – from rolls of barbed wire to cases of bullybeef – to the trenches.

Trench mortars were not new; the infantry had the Stokes mortars, a wonderful gun which rendered great service throughout the war. It was a fast-firing mortar, hurling bombs of several pounds in quick succession, but had only a short range. It also had the 'Plum Pudding', a round bomb about twelve inches in diameter with a steel shaft attached, also of short range and very useful for wire cutting to allow the infantry to pass through the entanglements in an attack.

The 'Flying Pigs' were not ready for issue so we 'cut our teeth' on the 'Plum Puddings', which we used to good effect in cutting a path for a raiding party in the Armentières sector.

Within a week or two we'd exchanged our 'Plum

Puddings' for our 'Flying Pigs'. They were impressive-looking weapons and their bomb – the Pig – stood about three feet high and looked more like a twelve-inch shell than a mortar bomb. The mortar looked like a squat howitzer and broke into several pieces for transport. Each piece weighed about 400 pounds and had rings attached through which to pass carrying poles for four men. The Flying Pigs had a range of about 1400 yards but, although they were reported to have proved a great success at Verdun, where in fortress conditions a solid bed could be found for them, we never had much success with them as, try as we might, we could never secure a firm bed to take the 'kick', which, because of the lack of any recoil mechanism, was great.

At Sanctuary Wood, at the apex of the Ypres salient, we made a bed of dozens of poles (that we had obtained often by dubious means) and driven down through the surface mud into solid earth. When we notified the Infantry in the trenches . . . of our intention to fire, they very wisely withdrew all men a hundred yards from each side of our line of fire. Our first shot must have landed on a German forward cook house, for our 'spotter' reported that the air was thick with galvanised iron and many cooking pots. Our next shot with exactly the same line and elevation landed some hundred yards to the left of the first one. Our gun bed had been knocked out of plumb. It was useless to persist so the mortar was dismantled and carried back to Dikkebus, two miles from Ypres, where the battery known as V2A was camped.

Notwithstanding our failure to get a bed from our numerous saplings, our sergeant impressed the C.O. of the 2nd Division, who, on a tour of inspection, stopped at our pit and admired the ingenuity displayed. Discovering that this was the sergeant's idea, [the officer] took him aside, and learning that he held an engineering degree from Melbourne University, had him commissioned within a few weeks and transferred to an artillery battery.

The sergeant's army career was to prove short-lived. He organised a football match with another division, stacked his team with Victorian League Players wherever he found them (other than the opposition) and could buy them with his ready cash – irrespective of battery, brigade or division – and backed them with IOUs for many hundreds of pounds. Of course they won in a canter but ninety per cent of those whom he had bet with woke up to the swindle and refused to pay up. The CO of his division took a very dim view of the affair and was reported as having spoken some very hard words to him. He got very tight that night, marched into the CO's bedroom, pulled him out of the bunk and punched him on the nose. Result: he was stripped of his rank, bowler-hatted and returned to Australia.

During July 1916 we moved, for the first time, to the Somme, where we took over a gun from the Pommies in the Chalk Pit, about one thousand yards from Pozières. It was out of range of the nearest German trench and, consequently, our job was to guard it and find a place to which we could move it. Although we were out of action, we received a good deal of attention from the German gunners but were well protected except from the left front, which was wide open. Fortunately, the Germans seldom fired at the Pit from that direction but, when he did, it was with heavy stuff, usually 5.9 howitzers. Unfortunately, he landed a shell on a bunch of our unit having their lunch of bullybeef and biscuits and killed them all. I was in the crew they had relieved the previous day.

It was a difficult time for the battery as in addition to guard duty at the Chalk Pit, we were continually searching, particularly in the direction of Mouquet Farm two miles from what had been Pozières, for places to install mortars to combat the German machine guns and trench mortars (minenwerfers) which were harassing our infantry and holding them up in their endeavours to capture the position. It was here that, for the first time since leaving it, I made contact with the 24th Battalion. A party of three of us had gone down Kay trench towards Mouquet Farm searching for positions to put in guns, but had little success. It was always difficult on a shell-torn battlefield to find such places. Our guns were too heavy for such work and they required solid ground to form a secure base to take the heavy recoil when fired. To find a suitable place was like looking for a needle in a haystack. The N.C.O. sent me back to the front line, if I could find it, to look for positions there. A gun could not be placed in the trench as it would form a block which would retard movement in it. The ideal spot was some twenty to thirty yards behind the line, preferably in a position from which it could destroy troublesome spots such as machine gun and minenwerfer posts. A large hole had to be dug for each gun – unless a suitable shell hole could be found (an unhealthy occupation) – and by then the infantry would have advanced and we were out of range. The Flying Pigs were, in effect, useless during an advance. There was no defined front line as represented by a trench, just a succession of loosely connected shell holes. I found myself on the edge of the cemetery (a particularly vicious spot) when I heard a well-remembered drawling voice say, 'Stand where you are for a few more seconds, Kyley, and you'll be dead', and there was an old friend from the 24th Battalion Bill Ward (an ex-Queensland cattle drover) crouching behind a broken tombstone. I very promptly joined him. It was good to meet him again under any conditions. He was a well-known character, tall, thin (but made of whipcord), laconic, kindly, but troublesome on the rare occasions he had one over the dozen. He wanted to know what I was doing in such a place and, when I told him, he advised me strongly to go back to the base as I would never find what I was looking for anywhere in the area, and, in any case, they were attacking that night in the first endeavour to take, or at least isolate, Mouquet Farm. If successful, the Germans would be out of range before we had a chance to get in a shot. Although an unhealthy place, I waited until it became dark to find my way back, where I reported the position to the Battery Commander and that, supported by the report of the N.C.O. who had been in charge of the party, put an end to any idea of putting a gun in. I only saw Bill once again, and that was in a somewhat similar situation on a later visit to the Somme. I have often wondered if he survived the war. I hope he did, he was of the type that made the A.I.F. the fighting force it had become.

The opposite number to the 'Flying Pig' was the German minenwerfer, of which they had thousands and which they used with great effect. The reasons they could do this were simple: their mortars were much lighter than ours, easier to handle, and, so we understood, had a recoil system and, as we were always moving forward over broken ground, whilst they invariably moved backwards to more solid ground, they were always able to bed their guns on solid bases. Many of them were of concrete and in carefully picked positions in, or close behind, the trenches they retreated to . . .

We headed back towards Belgium and moved about like gypsies for a while. No one apparently knew what to do with us; we were neither fish nor fowl. Our next move was far into Belgium, between Belgians on our left and French on our right, they being on the left of British–Australians troops who, in turn, were on the left of Ypres. We took over the position of a Belgian battery site which had been abandoned because too many of their shells fell short; that, at least, is what we were unofficially told. The Belgians had treated themselves well and had created weatherproof sloping huts and mess sheds. The weather improved and the days were full of sunshine. We had nothing to do and stayed there for, perhaps, three weeks.

The weather showing some improvement, we moved from the Belgian battery to a small ruined chateau in Ploegsteert Wood (the Old Tommy Plugstreet). The little chateau had been a gem and was reported to have been the hunting lodges of a Belgian nobleman (some said the German Crown Prince Little Willie).

Here we voted on the conscription issue and as a reward for assisting in the taking of the vote, I was given the job of carting the sealed bag with the votes to the collecting centre at Bailleul where, being stony broke, I could not buy myself even a beer.

Much has been said and written about the soldiers' votes against conscription. The reason was plain and simple. They were proud of their voluntary status and did not want it sullied by men who had to be conscripted. That attitude was proven wrong in the Second World War of 1939–45 when conscripts fought shoulder to shoulder with volunteers and showed that they could take it, and give it, with the best. They were all Australians.

The bitter fight between those wanting to keep Australia a volunteer army and those demanding recruitment be made compulsory proved to be the single most contentious public issue during the war. C. E. W. Bean, the war historian, called it *'a violent struggle in Australian political history.'*

Class and religious differences were very much a part of the conscription debate, with the mainly middle-class Protestants in favour of conscription and the largely working-class Catholics against it. Blue-collar workers pointed out they would be the bunnies and 'cannon fodder' rather than the white-collar workers who so sanctimoniously demanded conscription. Working-class women were especially against the idea of their sons being forced to fight in the war.

Within the first seven weeks at Gallipoli, the A.I.F. suffered 27,000 casualties and by the end of 1915 the number of men voluntarily enlisting couldn't make up the deficit. More men were needed desperately and conscription seemed to be the only answer.

The battle for and against conscription grew extraordinarily heated when the British Army Council demanded reinforcements from Australia and forcefully pointed out that Britain had introduced conscription in January 1916, that New Zealand had followed in June of the same year, and it was time for Australians to buck up and do what they were told.

Archbishop Mannix, the Catholic archbishop of Melbourne, openly declared himself anti-British and argued that the war was for the good of the British and would undermine Australia's future. A great many Catholics followed his lead and the battlelines were drawn. It was Catholics, the trade unions and working-class women versus the Press, Protestants, white-collar workers and all the state governments with the exception of Queensland. The paradox, of course, was that the war itself was never the issue, there was almost universal support among the whole population, Catholic and Protestant, for war.

A popular poster at the time urging conscription showed the evil Hun in his spiked helmet, blood dripping from the corners of his mouth as he attacked Australian women and children in their own backyard. Those wishing to keep the volunteer status fought back with a popular song, a single verse of which was often used as a short poem:

The Blood Vote

Why is your face so white, mother?
Why do you choke for breath?
Oh, I have dreamt in the night, my son
That I doomed a man to death!

Dame Nellie Melba, the greatest songbird of them all, campaigned vigorously for the blood vote, using the argument that if the Kaiser won the war the first nation he would want would be Australia. Why we would be the top priority on Germany's want list was never made clear. For those favouring conscription it was sufficient to know that Britain needed more men to fight, and if they wouldn't volunteer to do so, then they must jolly well be forced.

Today the concept of volunteering to go to war must seem absurd, but those were different times, and, surprisingly, a high percentage of the men fighting at the front voted against conscription. According to Bean, some of the reasons they gave were: *'nobody should be made to come to this'*, *'every man should be able to make up his own mind'* and *'if they have to be forced to come they won't be much good over here'*.

The issue of conscription was to be defeated in two separate referendums, the first narrowly and the second by a large majority. Nevertheless it continued to be a divisive issue and would leave scars that were to last up until World War II when conscription was introduced for service in New Guinea. Conscription was even raised in parliament at the beginning of the Vietnam War, where a compromise was quickly reached by introducing a lottery system.

Our following move was back to the Somme and an old camping ground at Mametz Wood, where we arrived in early autumn. The ground was a quagmire. My mate, Clive Talbot, one of the best of men from Birregurra in Victoria, and I scooped out most of the mud from a hole in the side of the rise, which had been the abode of some previous occupant, covered it with as much timber as we could find – or steal – tied down a waterproof sheet on top of that, fastened an old discarded greatcoat across the entrance to trap the light and keep out the cold, and were reasonably snug. The camp was not well situated for comfort. It was on a rise facing the front and, although several miles behind the line, was well within range of the larger calibre of German field guns; the one which worried us mostly was a nine-inch naval gun, which had such high velocity that you heard the explosion of the shell, perhaps half a mile away, before you heard the screech of the shell passing through the air. Fortunately, they were of such a low trajectory that, as the ground froze hard, many of them bounced off and ricocheted with a piercing scream until falling harmlessly to earth. None of them hit our camp area, although sometimes were uncomfortably close.

A word about Clive Talbot with whom I had formed a close friendship. Son of an old established Western District grazier, his property was known as 'Yeo Vale' and, following the old English custom, was entailed from father to eldest son (a practice now discarded). The entail was legally broken when Clive enlisted, which caused complications as he was later killed.

We were back on the labour guard again, this time mostly loading ammunition onto G.S. wagons for transport to forward batteries. After a couple of months I was granted ten days leave to Blighty (the U.K.) and arrived in London a day or two before Christmas 1916.

I had palled up with an artificer sergeant on the ferry across the channel and we booked into Faulkner's Hotel in Villiers Street, running down beside Charing Cross Railway

Station, to the embankment close by Cleopatra's Needle. The small hotel had been recommended to me by a friend in the battery who had made it his headquarters on his leave prior to mine. It was quite clean.

Before booking us in, the receptionist required production of our certificates declaring that we were free of vermin. We had to complete a questionnaire, one of the questions being 'Permanent Address', to which my companion answered 'Somme', much to the amusement of the receptionist.

Our first visit was to a barber where we each had a haircut, shave, shampoo, facial massage and electrical face and head massage – the lot. It was a wonderful experience and took about three hours of our precious time, but it was time and money well spent. The total cost was 12s 6d.

The next day or two we spent mainly in restaurants and theatres and viewing various landmarks of inner London.

It had always been my intention to endeavour to find Scottish connections when I obtained leave. My only clue was the knowledge that my great-grandfather and his family had come from Allanton/Allington in Larnarkshire, which a map disclosed was roughly between Glasgow and Edinburgh, and that my grandfather had worked on an estate of that name, Allanton, belonging to the Seton-Stewarts. Information later obtained was to the effect that he had leased land from that family.

The home of my grandparents in Geelong was named Allanton one year, Allington the next, and confusion arose from a difference of opinion between my grandparents, my grandfather claiming that it should be Allanton, my grandmother insisting that it should be Allington. My grandfather was, of course, correct but nothing could convince my grandmother . . .

My companion, deciding to come with me, arrived in Glasgow and booked into the Grand Hotel in Sauchiehall Street at a tariff of five shillings per day, which was the charge to all overseas servicemen. And they say the Scots are mean!

The Scots were certainly hospitable and the only way to remain reasonably sober was to declare yourself a teetotaller to all the offers of drinks from hotel meal guests.

It transpired that there was no train to Allanton, and there was no chance of car hire as cars were scarce and no petrol was available. I would probably have made efforts to get to Allanton by some means but it never stopped raining – pouring would be a better word. After two days my companion had had enough and returned to London. After another day, I followed him.

I travelled to Salisbury Plain where my brother, Len, was in training with his unit, the 39th Battalion of the 3rd Australian Division. My brother-in-law, Perce Bawdon, was also there with reinforcements for the 8th Battalion. Len obtained a couple of days leave and we spent Christmas Eve and Day together in London. I remember we saw a show at, I think, the Shaftesbury Theatre where the star billings were the Australians Fred Leslie and Joy Schelling in the *Spider and the Fly Dance* and that great Scottish comedian Harry Lauder, whose only child, Captain Lauder, had that day been on the casualty list amongst those killed. It must have been a frightful blow to him but Lauder carried on with his songs and jokes without a quiver. It was a wonderful show of courage and the audience rose at the end and stood for a minute in silence. Only then did he show any emotion and thanked them in a strangled voice for their sympathy and understanding.

I never saw Len again.

I had been in touch with people named Palmer of Iden (three miles from Rye in Sussex), connections of Uncle Albert Palmer, who was a member of the Federal Parliament and who during a visit to England on parliamentary business had given them my brother's address. Len had visited them during a leave and given them my address. They invited me to stay with them, an invitation which I accepted. They proved to be delightful people. I spent the next three days with them, mainly with a single and a married daughter who took me in hand.

The Palmer father, aged eighty-four, had gone to Australia shortly after the discovery of gold and claimed that he had the first weatherboard W.C. in Ballarat, where he conducted a pharmacy. Three brothers came out and promised that one of them would return at the end of three years. He, being the youngest, was chosen to go back. His intention was to become a surgeon and return to Australia but, in his own words, 'he got married instead' and opened a pharmacy in Hastings. He remained there until his retirement to Iden, where he built a home and named it 'The Bungalow'. One daughter, May, was married to an expatriate Scot,

George Tweedale, a farmer of 'Baron's Grange', Iden. It was them with whom I stayed. For three days I ate off good crockery on white linen and for four nights slept between white sheets. Time was running out and I transferred to the home of the eldest sister, married to a delightful elderly pharmacist of Lee (a London suburb) named Fairman. They were equally charming people . . .

Having exceeded my leave by two days, I reluctantly said goodbye and took the channel ferry from Folkestone to Boulogne and thence to Etaples, a mile or two away, which was the Australian base in France, where I had a piece of good fortune. There had been a fire in the orderly room on the day prior to my arrival and the base's current records had been destroyed. As a consequence, all the itinerants in the camp were mustered on parade and the sergeant-major started proceedings by calling out all those who had arrived there six days previously, and so down the scale, when, at No. 2 I stepped out, and was given a note to the effect that through no fault of my own I had been delayed at camp for two days. With this and a railway pass, I took a train to Amiens and from there by foot to Mametz Wood where I presented my note and all was well.

A couple of weeks later, we moved to Le Sars where I fell foul of authority. With one other I was ordered to dig a latrine trench for the officers. The very thought of such indignity repelled me (I was very young) and I refused to do it. I was paraded before the battery commander, who gave me the chance to recant, which I refused. He dismissed me with a dire warning of the consequences should I again appear before him. It was a foolish action on my part and, had I been a year or two older, it would not have happened.

Fatigue duty continued from our bases at Mametz Wood (but there was little sign of a wood) mostly on behalf of the infantry. We carted everything, from duckboards to semi-circular galvanised iron to support dugouts, into the front side of trenches, from ammunition to rolls of barbed wire. The galvanised iron was the worst. It had to be carried on your head (which greatly limited your view) along redoubted saps and trenches against oncoming fluently testy troops and often in a high wind on duckboards made slippery with frost.

The pattern continued through most of the 1916–17 winter, considered to be the worst winter on record, and certainly the worst during the war years. The temperature was frequently below zero and the ground was frozen as hard as iron. Try to drive a pick into it and you were in danger of the pick rebounding or of the impact numbing your arms. Water in shell holes was frozen into solid blocks.

During the worst of it, enquiries were made by the battery sergeant-major to find anyone who had driven a horse. Unsuspecting, I admitted that I had. I was told to report to the quartermaster-sergeant, who had a borrowed G.S. wagon hitched to a pair of mules. I had never handled, let alone driven, a mule but there was no getting out of it, so I picked up the reins and coaxed the mules to move off and away we went to pick up a load of rations. The road, which was over undulating country, was crowded with two and four mule-drawn wagons carting stores of all sorts to the forward zone in anticipation of the spring offensive. To add to the confusion, the odd Vauxhall staff car carried anything from generals to lieutenants resplendent in red and gold, and all were very irate and seemingly unaware that their own penchant to travel on the wrong side of the road was the cause of their delays.

Mules going up a rise would spend as much time on their knees on the frozen slippery surface of the road as they did on their feet. Those going down had their legs slip from under them and simply sat on their behinds and slid downwards, accelerated by the weight of the wagon with brakes hard on. The result was chaotic.

We finally finished our loading, and with a couple of stiff O.P. rum inside us, provided by a sympathetic quartermaster, we set out for 'home'.

Somehow or other we came through with only minor cuts to knees and the skimmed backsides of our pair of mules and a broken spoke of two of our G.S. wagon. The Q.M. sergeant always claimed that Ben Turpin's ride was nothing compared to our drive.

The only event of note at this place was the dropping of an unusual bomb – if such it could be called – by a low-flying German plane. It landed about a foot or eighteen inches from the back wall of the hut along which I was lying on my bunk. It made only a 'phut' on explosion, but created a small crater that extended under my bunk. Pieces of the shell we found were made up of lead. It created great interest, and red-and-gold-splashed staff officers appeared the following day. They had no answer to the riddle, but my opinion is that it was a toy bomb put together by a German with a sense of humour.

Sometime in January 1917, we were to learn that we had been chosen to destroy the Butte-de-Warlencourt. The butte was a hillock on the northern slope of a valley which the Germans had made into a veritable fortress. It was like a beehive of concrete machine gun, field gun and mortar emplacements capped by a high concrete blockhouse, which was impregnable to any available gun fire; shells either exploded harmlessly or bounced off it.

On the opposite southern side of the valley was the ruined village of Warlencourt, on the same road and about 800 yards from the butte.

Our first objective was to find a cellar in which to install our mortar – the 'Flying Pig'. That was no easy task because the Germans looked down on the village so we could only move about there at night, and then no more than three at a time.

The village was really a No Man's Land. We could not occupy it because of the dominance of the butte. The Germans were happy to stay where they were and, I suppose, hope that we would be silly enough to try and cross the valley. Our only light was from the flares thrown up by both sides, particularly the German who kept a watchful eye on the village. Consequently our search was spasmodic, as each time a flare went up we had to take whatever cover was handy or, if that was not possible, to freeze and hope you looked as much like a piece of broken masonry as possible. The only way to find a cellar was to fall into one, and that is what happened when one night one of our searchers fell into a cellar that had a large hole in its roof, through which had fallen most of the building which it had served.

Firstly, we had to seal the cellar against possibility of any glimmer showing through. To do this, we required several long pieces of timber and, failing to find any amongst the ruins, we had to beg, borrow or steal them wherever we could and carry them up at night, together with some old rusty scraps of iron. It was a race against time to get them into position and covered with rubble before daylight. That being accomplished, all we had to do to make it light-proof and practically airproof was to hang blankets as curtains, one at the bottom of the stairs and one about a yard up the stairs. Candles being unprocurable, we had to make do with tins of fat, obtained from the cook, in which floated wicks made from ropes. They gave off little light but lots of black sooty smoke.

Three of us worked there and three on top for a couple of weeks. The first night we sent up enough rubble in sand bags to cover our makeshift roof. The heavy pieces of masonry had to be broken into manageable sizes and weights, and passed to the men on top, who would search out a place to dump it that was not likely to be spotted by Fritz. The rubble was shovelled into sandbags and emptied in similar places. It was slow work as, half the time, the top men were immobile because of flares, and the stuff had to be dumped over a large area.

The cellar having been cleared, we were ready to install

the mortar and, hopefully, blow the butte and all in and on it into oblivion. When the Germans pulled back to prepared positions beyond Bapaume, we were left with a useless ex-fortress, very adequately destroyed and, like the forts at Singapore in a later war, facing the wrong way.

It was fortunate for us that the Germans left before we disclosed our position as, whether or not we had succeeded in destroying the fort, they would have destroyed us, our flimsy roof offering little or no protection.

One result of our incarceration in the cellar was that the six of us coughed up what looked like tar for several days until it began to slowly improve – the result of the sooty smoke given off by our makeshift lamps.

We immediately found ourselves laden with our heavy mortars and a couple of push-carts loaded with bombs, on the main road from Albert to Bapaume, going nowhere. The night was bitterly cold and the road slippery and pockmarked with shell holes. Our officers had no idea whether the German was a hundred yards or miles ahead and for several hours we marched up and down that road under constant heavy artillery fire. At daylight we found a railway culvert and were sound asleep in seconds. It was one of the worst nights of my experience. During our perambulations we had passed backwards and forward, through Bapaume on at least two occasions. It was burning but there was no sign of the Germans.

It was from about this time that my memory of places and events and their sequence are, in general, dimmed in comparison with the previous two years. I have often thought about this over the years and am satisfied that it was due to war weariness, both physical and mental. It is impossible to convey in words the hopelessness of our position. We never doubted that we would eventually win the war, but every front-line soldier who survived it for years must have had grave doubts as to whether he would be alive at the end, unless that came suddenly, and there was no indication of that occurring.

Pictures – and there have been millions of them – do convey to some extent the horror of the war but only those who have actually experienced it can fully understand the immensity of it; the deadening effect on the mind of an enemy artillery barrage that may go on for hours when all around you the earth is being tortured and convulsed by continuous explosions of shells which have buried themselves in the earth, while others, with instantaneous fuses, are bursting on impact with the ground, hurling large and small fragments of steel in all directions. Yet other shells burst overhead and hurl steel balls of fragments of jagged steel downward. Added to all this is the deadly clatter of machine guns and the crack of rifle fire, the whine of bullets and the screech of the shells as they descend overhead to explode in front of you or behind your trench or shelter. Amidst all this, you huddle to the front wall of the trench or whatever cover there is, no matter how small. You know that your friends are dying or, if lucky, have been wounded whilst you wait for your turn and hear above the din the constant call for stretcher bearers.

If you are very lucky you come out of such a hell physically untouched but mentally dead.

Such is the resilience of the human mind that, physically removed to softer conditions, you soon recover your normal powers of thought and behaviour, but you don't lose the belief that you will go once too often to the front line, and each time you go, you wonder whether it will be the last.

We were not, of course, always under barrage, but during our battles in the Somme area they were constant, and the cumulative effect was to deaden the minds of those who took part in them. Our resolve, however, to see it through never weakened. We lost all faith in the teachings of the Church, politicians and, to a lesser extent, the army, that God was on our side and that we were fighting a war to end wars.

The feelings of the troops are portrayed in a humorous story claimed to have come from George Bernard Shaw, the great wit and humorist of the times, who said that when passing a church one Sunday morning he was feeling very depressed by the war news, he decided to seek solace inside. Being an atheist, he had not been inside a church for many years. He did not get any relief from the service and said that he emerged convinced that God was a glorified colonel with the British army.

One evidence of the hardening (or coarsening) effect on our minds and outlook of the kind of warfare we were involved in was discernible in our attitude to death. When, in earlier days, the death of a mate would have been a tragedy, it was now met with 'poor bastard, he was a good mate' or words to that effect. The feeling was there but dulled.

It became a case of 'who cracked first' and, fortunately, it was the Germans. Not that we showed any sign of cracking, but the human mind and body can only take so much; it is not inexhaustible.

Sometime into the spring of 1917, we were taken back to Le Sars for a spell. We had been there a few days only when I was ordered to report to Battery H.Q. The C.O. Captain Heath – in civilian life a jeweller, one of the members of the family who owned Gaunts in Bourke Street, Melbourne – advised me that I had been chosen to attend a signalling school at Flesselles, about ten kilometres north of Amiens. I told him I had no desire to be a signaller. He replied that he had no place for a signaller but had been instructed to send two of the battery to the school and, as it appeared that I had been in the line more than most, he had chosen me and one other to give us a good spell. So we made our way to Flesselles and Madame Edouard.

We were told that we were to be billeted with Madame Edouard and, following instructions, found her ancient but solid cottage. Like Madame, it was small and old and, although there may have been other rooms, the only ones occupied were a huge slate-paved kitchen and Madame's bedroom which opened off it. In three corners of the kitchen were three built-in beds of mammoth proportions and great depth. There were small step-ladders attached to each bed and, having climbed over and in, you sank into about two feet of feather mattress, filled with the pluckings of many generations. The result was stifling but, on a cold night, wonderfully warm.

Madame was a character, full of fire, and always, apparently, in a rage, but she had a vast heart. We handed her our rations and she gave us breakfast and dinner on a white cloth, providing fresh vegetables from her own little patch all for ten francs each per week (it appeared to be the standard charge).

My mate was a quiet but pleasant youth about my own age named Maddox and, because of his hair, known as Snowy. The third bunk was, at the weekends, occupied by Madame's pretty daughter, aged about twenty-five, who worked in an ammunitions factory some kilometres away. She had no inhibitions and undressed in the light from an open fireplace while we pretended not to be looking. Madame, however, was alert and any movement, such as going out to relieve oneself, would bring her to the door in a flash.

We learnt morse code and how to operate the buzzer, flags and the light. We had to signal one to the other at a distance of 500 yards. In the early stages we would signal the names of cities and, as there were Tommies at the school, a favourite with the Australians was 'WOOLLOOMOOLOO'. It completely bamboozled the Tommies.

Madame never appeared to stop talking. (We named her Madame Machine Gun.) Even when she was on her own, you could hear her pitched staccato voice angrily denouncing someone or something. One evening as the light was fading, I could hear her spitting fire from the direction of her backyard. I found her dancing like a whirling dervish and shrieking what sounded like obscenities in French at an unfortunate British airman, who headed for home at full throttle, with a German on his tail pouring a string of machine-gun bullets at him. There was little our man could do and his only hope appeared to be that the German would run out of ammunition before he registered a hit. Madame continued her war dance until both planes disappeared behind a hill. In what little French I could muster, I tried to pacify her and explain that the British airman had no chance to do anything but run for cover, but the only response was a scornful 'He run like a lapin! He run like lapin!'

Dear old toothless, unlovely, indomitable, vinegary Madame Edouard. She had the spirit that makes countries great, and we loved her.

All good things come to an end and, having passed out as fully fledged signallers, we made our way back to the battery, and soon forgot all we had learnt.

Apart from Madame Edouard, the only memory of Flesselles that lingers is of the delightful custard tarts which we used to buy from the local baker as he extracted them with his long-handled wooden scoop from the oven built into the side of an earthen wall.

Following on our now established pattern, we continued as hod carriers to the infantry, digging saps and carting and laying duckboards to the front in the preparation for the Messines attack which was preceded by, up to that time, the world's greatest manmade explosion that practically eliminated a ridge. Our side had tunnelled for many months to accomplish the task and, having succeeded, the infantry were forced to watch the Germans in full flight, the artillery bringing up their horses and galloping away with the guns. There was a total lack of imagination in the High Command. The pattern had been established. You blasted the German with everything you had and then, having reached the objective set for you, you halted and dug in, no matter what condition he was in. It was not until the Australian Corps came under the command of their own brilliant General Monash that, conditions being satisfactory, the attacking troops were encouraged to go forward and reap the reward for their victory by gaining extra ground and killing more of the enemy.

A couple of months after my return to the battery, I made an application to join the Australian Flying Corps then being formed. The C.O., Major Seymour, took a personal interest in this and was certain his recommendation would clinch it. Within a few days I had been called to an interview in a town some distance away. There, apart from many probing questions and a medical examination, I had to ride a bicycle and stand on one leg on a kitchen chair, first with my eyes open and then with them closed. To my astonished query as to what it all meant, I was told that it was to test my balance. Planes of the day were certainly flimsy affairs but I never could understand why to ride in one you had to be able to stand on a chair on one leg, with or without eyes closed, and ride a bike. Shortly after this interview I became ill with grossly swollen joints in my hands, knees, hips and shoulders. I had contracted the dreaded trench fever.

Major Seymour visited me daily and urged me to hang on as he was sure that the call would come for me. After some days I had to be carried away on a stretcher; and so to a Yankee Hospital at Camiers (which I think was near Boulogne, but I was too sick to bother about it), where I was diagnosed as suffering from acute arthritis. I told them I was suffering from trench fever, but they had only been a week or two in France and had never heard of it. There was one Yankee patient in the hospital with a hundred or two Tommies and Australians. I understand there was an Australian hospital in the vicinity which was full of Yankees. Such is the inscrutable wisdom of the army! I don't know whether or not Australian doctors officially recognised such an ailment as trench fever but I am certain that they did unofficially. The troops had no doubts about it.

The nurses were lovely women, kind and sympathetic, and handled us with tender care. The Yankee doctors were in a different mould – unsympathetic to the point of callousness. As an illustration: there was a little Aussie in the bed next to me with a knee as big as a head. He had collected a number of bomb splinters around the knee and had lain out in No Man's Land, very close to the German trenches, for three days before our people managed to rescue him. By the time he reached a forward dressing station, the knee had swollen and turned green. By the time it was decided to operate, it was a horrible mixture of pus and green.

One morning, screens were erected around his bed and the sole Yankee patient (who was a nephew of the Carnegie of steel fame and had lost a leg) played on his portable recorder a new record that had been sent to him from the U.S.A. – 'The Missouri Waltz'. It was, he said, sweeping the

States. When he saw the screens he tucked his machine and record under one arm, his crutch under the other and, remarking that he 'had seen this before', headed for the open air.

The operation was to draw off fluid from underneath the kneecap. To do this without any anaesthetic, meant a few people had to hold him down while others checked under his knee cap with a hollow probe with which they hoped to draw the liquid by attaching it to a vacuum flask. The language of the digger had to be heard to be believed and, after failing in their attempt, a doctor remonstrated with him for using such language before the nurses. His response was unforgettable. 'You bastard, I would give everything I possess, or am ever likely to possess, to get you on the other end of that bloody thing.' The next day they took his leg off; this time with chloroform.

After several days I was shipped off to England, whereupon on arrival, I was placed on a train which took me to Connaught Hospital, Aldershot, where an English doctor demanded to know what I was doing there. He riled me and I assured him no one had asked me where I wanted to go, and, if they had, Aldershot was the last place I would have chosen.

I spent several days there, during which I got on my feet, and at the weekend I joined a party from the hospital to have tea and scones at the home at Farnborough of the ex-Empress Eugenie of France, whose husband, Napoleon III, had abdicated after the debacle of the 1871 war with

Germany. She was a dear little old lady, who, supported by two ladies, totted around her lovely garden and had a few words with each of us. She died a year later and I am probably one of the few people alive who can claim to have met her.

After several days, I was transferred to the Australian hospital at Dartford, about twenty miles from London, where I found my second cousin, Ruby Ripper, in charge of a ward to which she arranged to have me transferred.

Ruby was a fine and beautiful woman and, although it was against the rules and regulations for a commissioned officer – she was a captain – to fraternise with private soldiers she claimed that they did not apply to cousins. Occasionally we would slip into Dartford by a path known to mobile troops, leaving and returning without a pass (the entry into the hospital grounds was through a hole in the enclosing fence) for a cup of tea at the 'George', a lovely old coaching inn. Ruby married a Canadian and after the war joined him on his farm, which I believe was near Montreal.

I saw several London theatrical shows while stationed here. The 'hole in the wall' helped and, being less than an hour by train, it was easy to see a show and be back by midnight.

My health showed steady improvement and about mid-October, I went to a convalescence depot at Hurdcott on Salisbury Plain, and it was here that I learnt of the deaths in action at Passchendaele, Belgium, of my brother, Len, and brother-in-law, Percy Bawden.

I had visited an old 24th Battalion friend in another row

when I was halted by, 'Hey, is your name Kyle?' coming from a man standing in the lighted doorway of a hut. He then asked if I was a brother of Len Kyle. I replied in the affirmative and when I asked if he knew anything of Len, adding that I had not heard from him for some time, he replied, 'You will never see Len again.' I was floored and made my way back to my hut without any further comment.

I called the following day and met the man from Len's battalion, the 39th, and he told me Len was missing at Passchendaele. A few weeks later, letters from home told me of my brother-in-law's death, which was eight days before Len's death.

They worked us hard to get us fit at Hurdcott, up at daylight, on parade ground often for the best part of an hour, jogging, physical jerks and a quick march for a mile or two. Back to camp for a hot breakfast, then more drill, bayonet practice and physical jerks until a good hot lunch, mainly lectures during the afternoon until four, when you were free to wander the countryside and visit such 'flesh-pots' as comforts, Y.M.C.A. or Salvation Army huts to fraternise with friends or acquaintances over tea and buns. A dull life, but a healthy one which increased my weight to twelve stone for the first time in my life, and not an ounce of fat on it.

Towards the end of January, I was passed fit for active service and transferred to the staging camp at Longbridge, Deverell, where we drilled and marched as much as ever and went through various exercises, such as passing through sealed chambers filled with lachrymatory and chlorine gases to test our gas helmets. Apparently, if the helmet leaked in the former, you cried, if in the latter, you died.

Early in February 1918, I went on ten days' leave prior to returning to France and spent it between Tweedales (Palmers) and Fairmans in London, where I saw a number of good theatrical productions, mostly musical comedies, visited the National Art Gallery, the British Museum, Ye Olde Cheshire Cheese (where I dined on Yorkshire Pudding and sat in Dr Johnson's chair), dined at Simpsons in the Strand (where I ate prime English beef at the table from a roast, wheeled from table to table in a silver barrow), visited Dirty Dick's and Madame Tussaud's, The Old Curiosity Shop, the zoo, Hampton Court, Westminster, London Bridge and other places of interest . . . Looking back on it from this distance in time, I wonder how all this was done in five or six days. It seems impossible but you cram a lot into a short time when you are young and healthy and life may be very short and your guide and mentor is a Londoner born and bred such as Charles Fairman, who knew every part of it.

There were two zeppelin air raids during this short time. In the first raid, they were after the vast ammunitions factory at Greenwich, about two miles from the Fairmans' home, and we had a good view of one airship, like a golden cigar in the glow of the search lights. The second raid was while Mrs Fairman and I were viewing a musical comedy – it may have been *High Jinks* – at, I think, the Adelphi Theatre in the Strand. I felt a great pride in being of British descent when the leading man (Jack Buchanan it may have been) came out on the stage and calmly announced that

'There's likely to be a little fun from up above shortly. We are going to carry on. Are you?' and not a single person moved from his or her seat, although bombs (500 pounders) fell perilously close, one cutting the building housing Horatio Bottomley's *John Bull* newspaper into two within 200 yards of the theatre.

I had a wonderful twelve days and very reluctantly returned to camp, where I was punished for overstaying my leave.

Towards the end of February, I was sent to France. From Etaples I was posted to an artillery transport unit, which was a practice in the artillery with men who had been absent from their units for an extended period, presumably to allow time for H.Q. to find out if there was room for you in your old unit and if they wanted you back. The response in my case must have been favourable as, after about a week, I was told I should rejoin the battery in the Armentières sector.

Life in the transport unit had mixed blessings. It was bitterly cold but the huts in which we lived were almost cosy. The mules were the main drawback. They are without doubt, the most contrary animals imaginable. They are also very dangerous to handle, as anyone will know who has had anything to do with a line of about thirty of them, rugged and tethered along a country lane full of ice puddles, and with a freezing stream about six feet behind them. They kick and paw at the fence or at each other until their rugs are loose and hanging underneath their bellies. You are kept busy putting the rugs back in position, tightening girths and untangling front legs from halters while they do their best to paw or bite you or, what is worse, to kick you into the frozen stream. Unlike a horse, which kicks kindly and with one leg at a time, the mule carefully measures the distance and then plants its hoofs with all the power and expertise of a champion boxer delivering a knock-out punch.

I had never handled mules (other than the pair I mentioned earlier) so they must have gloated when I turned up. At any rate, one of them succeeded on my first night of line duty and kicked me into the icy stream. Fortunately, I saw it coming and turned my back in time to have both hooves planted on my backside, and suffered nothing more than a badly bruised behind and a very cold dunking. The sergeant on duty took me into his shelter, where there was a coal-fired brazier, and I was able to strip, wrap myself in a blanket, and dry out my clothes.

Although on line duty for most of the several nights I was with the unit, I had learnt my lesson and kept a wary eye on the mules. To do this successfully you had to watch their eyes, not their legs, and whenever they eyed you from the front, or turned their heads to look at you, you promptly took evasive action.

On return to the battery I missed my mate Clive Talbot and, although I had a number of good friends, never again did I have such a close mate.

The same old routine was in operation – in the line and out again in perpetuum, with the odd fatigue job intervening. One I remember since it showed me how easy it would be to die in the snow. It happened like this:

It was bitterly cold and the ground was covered with a

foot or more of snow. We carried sheets of galvanised iron curved to half a circle to support dugouts cut into the side of the trenches and to keep them dry of seepage. We were supporting the 6th Brigade and had to pass along the front line occupied by, I think, the 21st Battalion. After depositing our burden, a tall dark-haired officer, who turned out to be Soss Wertheim, a well-known Melbourne man-about-town and famous tennis player, took pity on us and poured out a liberal spot of overproof rum from his water bottle for each of us. Our return to base took us along a duckboarded path cut into the side of a hill. I was the last of the line and, with the combined effect of the rum on an empty stomach and the cold and physical exhaustion, it became impossible to drag one foot after the other and I more or less collapsed into the snow on the high side of the track. I had a feeling of warmth and contentment as the snow wrapped around me (helped, no doubt, by the rum) and promptly fell into a deep sleep, from which I was woken by two of the party who had come back to search for me. After a few hundred yards we came to a Salvation Army shelter, where I had a cup of coffee, and the S.A. man offered me a bunk for the night, which I gladly accepted. He provided a warm breakfast before I returned to the battery . . . The Salvation Army . . . has had my support ever since.

We returned to base later in the day and, to our delight, found that the battery was to be broken up, most of us forming a new battery to be known as the 'Fourth Medium Trench Mortar Battery' and the balance, with their useless mortars, to become Corp troops. The new unit was to be issued with a new mortar known as the Newton-Stokes, firing a twenty-eight-pound bomb. Volunteers were called for and I said goodbye to the Flying Pig which, but for one occasion, never flew.

The next few weeks were spent familiarising ourselves with the new mortars and, at about the end of February 1918, we took our mortars into action in the Noreuil sector, with our base at Vaux. We were, I think, successful and the infantry appeared to be pleased, which was a change since we had never been popular with them as we had always been looking for, and never found, a place from which we could operate.

It would have been towards the end of March 1918 that we moved to the Somme for the second time. Remembering our first experiences, it was not an enticing prospect. This time, however, we travelled in style in an old London doubledecker motor bus, the first and last time I travelled in comparative comfort during my service.

Despite the hurry to get us there we had an inauspicious arrival at our destination – Amiens. The Germans had broken through the British in the Somme area and were threatening Amiens, having passed Albert – with its gilded hanging Virgin on the tower of its ruined church – and were within a few miles of Amiens. The breakthrough had been complete.

Although our mortars were a great improvement on the Flying Pig, they were too cumbersome to be useful in open warfare, and we were, accordingly, moved to Bèttencourt, several miles north-west of Amiens. The village had been badly damaged but its lovely chateau was untouched except for a shell at the front iron gates, another halfway up the drive, and still another just below the stone steps leading to the front door – remarkable shooting which gave the impression that they were placed there as a warning. Perhaps the marchioness had relatives or pre-war friends with authority amongst the Germans. In any case, she had taken the warning and had left without delay for safer climes. The only civilians we could find were two old retainers at the chateau and, as it looked to be the best boarding house in town, we promptly moved in – officers to the front, other ranks elsewhere.

Few, if any, of us had ever been in such a place. It was majestic, with vast reception areas and dining rooms, and the library was breathtaking. It was full of priceless treasures; paintings by old masters, a room full of silver to rival Aladdin's Cave and magnificent furniture, not to mention carpets and rugs obviously of great value, but the greatest treasure was the labyrinthine cellars which we later learned contained over 10,000 bottles of rare wine which were regarded as one of the finest collections in France. (It may have been Europe.) We soon discovered where the keys to the cellar were kept and enjoyed her ladyship's unintended hospitality. On the whole, we treated the treasures as they deserved to be treated and, for our small lapses, consoled ourselves with the thought that what little we took was as nothing to what the Germans would have taken had they got there first.

Our revelry lasted for three days when a car arrived, carrying two French staff officers resplendent in red and gold,

followed by a light wagon with five gendarmes, who immediately commenced guard duty on the cellars. The officers
departed, but obviously by pre-arrangement with our C.O.,
returned without warning and everybody was immediately
ordered on parade with full equipment. The rooms we occupied were then searched and various odds and ends of silver
collected and placed under guard.

That was bad enough but our indignation was soon
snuffed out when Tiny Rice, a very large Queenslander of
about six feet two and weighing around fifteen stone, was
ordered to undo his bulging tunic and numerous pieces of
silver, including a teapot, clattered to the ground, quickly
followed by another collection after his trousers were
undone. On being asked to explain, Tiny blandly replied
that he had no idea how they had got there, which was too
much for even the French officers, who yelled with laughter. Tiny got off with a warning as stern as their twitching
faces would allow.

A couple of days later, a convoy of heavy trucks took
away the contents of the cellars and, on subsequent trips,
those of the chateau . . .

In the meantime, we had been put to work dismantling a
hangar on an aerodrome on the outskirts of the village
which had been abandoned by the British, who had left
behind two or three planes that had apparently been
brought in for repair, as well as several aeroplane engines in
their crates.

The Germans had partially dismantled the hangar for us
and, before the job was completed, we were transferred to

the Villers-Bretonneux sector, where we operated for some weeks. At this time, the position was confusing and we were continually shifting our mortars wherever we were needed. Although everything was topsy-turvy, it was an exhilarating period as, for the first time, we felt that we were really winning, despite the determination of the Germans to knock that belief sky-high.

Australians had always fought well but never better than at this period when they stopped the Germans in their headlong thrust on Amiens. Years of service on Gallipoli, in Egypt and in the battles and front-line duties in France had moulded them into a disciplined, imaginative force unsurpassed by trained attacking forces in any of the combatant armies. Their original ranks had been sadly thinned but there always remained a core of old hands on which to rebuild shattered units, and new hands rapidly became old hands in the crucible that was France. They fought magnificently three months later also when they broke the famed Hindenburg Line, but I was not there to participate in that effort which prefaced the closing stages of the war.

It would have been in late May or early June that we transferred to Heilly on the Ancre, from where we operated in the Menicourt and Treux areas. The fighting here was constant and often fierce.

Our billets in Heilly were on a ford over the Ancre and it was not a healthy place. I occupied a cell, one of several along a long wing of the main building . . . with a friend named Reg Hinwood. One evening, just as dusk was falling, I was writing home and Reg was cleaning his rifle when the

German opened with a battery of 4.5 howitzers. One shell of the first salvo landed on our roof and I collected several pieces of it and Reg got other bigger ones. I missed most of the falling ceiling, roof timbers and walls but Reg was buried under them. I was blinded with a mixture of blood, debris and dust, having collected a small splinter in my right eyebrow, but some of my mates helped me across a courtyard and down into a cellar where the bulk of the men slept when off gun duty. I enquired as to the fate of Reg and that was their first intimation that he was still in the remains of our quarters. They immediately cleared away the rubble covering him and put him on a stretcher. Whilst being carried across the courtyard, one of his legs became badly gashed by a piece of shell exploding in the courtyard. The men carrying him miraculously escaped injury. His leg was saved and he returned to the battery only to lose it a few weeks later when, riding a stray mule for the fun of it, the mule kicked an unexploded shell buried an inch or two underground. The shell exploded, killing the mule and taking off Reg's leg completely this time. Reg was a very powerful and healthy young man, and within two days of losing his leg, was getting about on crutches. I heard later that he had died of T.B. some two years after his return to Australia.

An hour or two later we – me, Reg and another friend – were carried to a rendezvous (how we made it I do not know) with an ambulance and passed through Amiens, which was being heavily shelled, to an advanced Australian hospital, which was full of holes from a bombing attack the previous day, resulting in a number of casualties amongst staff (including two nurses being killed) and patients.

Conditions were primitive, the hospital being entirely under canvas, but the staff, doctors, nurses, orderlies and local French cleaning women were wonderfully kind. The nurses looked tired and old beyond their years, but were untiringly kind, attentive and cheerful.

In the bed next to me was the third member of the party, whose skull was laid open and brain exposed. He was delirious and every time anyone approached his bed he ordered them away in language which would have shocked a team of bullock drivers. It was embarrassing and, in apologising to the ward sister, I explained to her that normally he was one of the most gentlemanly men I had known . . . She told me that the language did not worry her or the other sisters as they had learned from long experience that, of the men suffering severe head wounds, the most decent became the most profane. Poor Bluey, I heard later that he died before he could be moved to a hospital in the rear.

Conditions were rough and ready. Gaping wounds had iodine poured into them and others were dabbed with it and the lot bandaged. My wounds became painful and I was given injections; more than the doctor ordered I was told, but the sisters were merciful and swore me to secrecy.

I am not sure how long I was in this hospital, perhaps two or three days, when I was moved to another US hospital near Rouen. Here my wounds, other than my head, were cleaned and re-bandaged. For some reason, which I never discovered, they refused to clean my head and left it bandaged . . .

I was here for ten to twelve days before I was shipped to England and to the British 1st Southern General Hospital in the buildings of the University of Birmingham at Edgebaston, a suburb of that city.

Here my head bandages were removed for the first time, but only after I complained of the intolerable itch. There was enough rubble in my hair to make a mud pie.

I had been there for some days when it was discovered that I had a dropped wrist, due to the severing of the median nerve and ligament in my right arm. I had no power in my wrist or feeling in my hand. As an experiment one day, I put the burning end of a cigarette on the back of my hand, felt no pain and only took it away when I smelt burning flesh.

The ward I was in had been the assembly hall, a vast place with an organ at one end, which I was told was the second-largest organ in the world. Whether or not it was true I do not know.

An organist . . . played to all who cared to listen two or three times a week, playing all the popular tunes of the day, including ragtime. It was amazing to hear rag played on such a vast instrument.

I stayed here for about three weeks and was then moved to the Australian Hospital at Dartmouth, where I found my second cousin, Ruby Ripper, who again had me moved to her ward.

The hospital was not very attractive, being long rows of low weatherboard buildings, each one comprising a ward. Its great advantage was its proximity to London, eighteen to twenty miles away, to which after the first few days I travelled two or three nights a week for a meal and a theatre, returning through the 'hole in the wall' referred to earlier. There were, of course, passes granted from time to time and Ruby appeared to have considerable influence with the 'base wallahs' who zealously controlled such privileges, and she kept me supplied with one every week or ten days. She was a trump.

Shortly after admission to hospital I had been operated on by a major – later a sir – a noted Melbourne surgeon assisted by a well-known Melbourne physician. My severed ligament and nerve were repaired, and I made rapid progress, regained lost weight and was ready in a few weeks to move on. All good things must come to an end!

I again moved to Hurdcott on Salisbury Plain, about six miles from Wilton and twelve from Salisbury. Long rows of Nissen huts again. The routine here was very much the same as my last visit, consisting of physical jerks and marches around the countryside with the odd day of leave into Salisbury, a dull town and certainly not worth the twenty-four-mile trudge, unless one was lucky enough to get a ride in a passing army vehicle.

CHAPTER 14

Going Home

In mid-August (1918), I was transferred to Weymouth Convalescent depot for troops awaiting transfer to Australia. Life was very dull here. Most of the troops were walking wounded, or weak from illness, and, consequently, duties were light. Weymouth was a dull town, although the surrounding countryside was attractive, which was poor solace for men longing to get home.

The war was going very well for us and it was obvious that the end was approaching. The advent of the U.S.A. into the war had given the allied command the reserves they required to sustain a constant offensive. They (the Yanks) arrived late on the scene and that, and not their actual fighting, was their greatest contribution to the allied victory. They fought well and bravely but their fighting involvement can be judged by their casualties – approximately the same as Australia's.

Early in October, I was given ten days' pre-embarkation leave which was spent mainly between Tweedales at Iden and Fairmans at Lee. They were really fine people and it was a privilege to know them . . .

It is a quirk of human nature that, although we lived with death during those terrible years, we never really believed it would affect us individually, or those dear to us.

Len and Percy and Clive Talbot and millions of others (including civilians) were grand and wanted nothing more than to live their lives in peace. The same could be said of all but an infinitesimal number of men and women on both sides, yet for four and a quarter years, we did our best to exterminate each other in all sorts of horrible ways, succeeding to the grand total (us and them) of 27,530,700 killed, wounded and missing, not counting the millions of civilians who suffered the same fate.

It was so senseless and largely due to national rivalry brought about by national pride and a few ambitious men on both sides, but mainly Germans, led by their Kaiser, the grandson of our Queen Victoria. It should have been possible for leading men on both sides to work out an honourable solution before the guns began to fire. There were many Germans of all ranks who disliked and mistrusted the Kaiser and his henchmen and there were others of high rank and importance whom it should have been possible to talk to, but once the war machines began to roll, national pride took over and insanity came into its own.

The great slogan preached by our leaders was that 'It was

a war to end all wars' and, as that was what we wanted to believe, we believed it.

Within twenty years, the same slaughter of the next generation began all over again, but this time there was no other way out. German Nazism, an illegitimate product of the Versailles Peace Treaty, had to be destroyed.

On 29 September 1918 the allies pierced the Hindenburg Line and Germany had finally had enough. Her allies were collapsing and German troops were refusing to fight and there were several mutinies reported in units at the front. Back home there were strikes and revolts and it became apparent that her people had lost their taste for war. As a nation, Germany was exhausted and furthermore it had changed from an autocracy to a republic. The new Weimar Republic was anxious to change the agenda created by the Kaiser and his old-guard generals and were keen to halt the hostilities and to sue for peace. On 4 October 1918 Germany sent a request to President Wilson to end the war. The thinking behind the approach to the Americans, the latecomers in the conflict, was that they might not prove as bitter as the British or the French and would be more likely to negotiate better terms for any future peace treaty. The Americans, possibly influenced by Britain and France, proved reluctant to take on the role of peacemakers and eventually Germany negotiated the armistice with France.

In the five weeks between the approach to the Americans and the eventual armistice, even though the British knew that Germany was willing to capitulate and lay down her arms, General Haig gave orders to his commanders to *'go on hitting (the enemy) hard . . .'til he begs for mercy'*. Given the opportunity to save lives, Haig once again showed how careless he was with them. This totally unnecessary and spiteful demand cost a further 100,000 British casualties. It seemed to the Germans that Britain, even though she had lost fewer men than the French, seemed to be more the vengeful of the two allies and so they chose who they thought was the lesser of the two evils. This proved to be a very big mistake. It was the French who wanted their revenge, not only because they lost the largest number of men in the war but also because in 1871 Germany 'stole' Alsace-Lorraine from France who was forced to pay Germany huge reparations to get it back. Nations tend to have long memories and now it would be Germany's turn to pay.

There were three requirements for the armistice:

- Immediate cessation of the war
- That the German forces be withdrawn behind the Rhine within thirty days
- The surrender of the German fleet and all heavy guns.

The Germans agreed to these conditions and the fighting officially ended with an armistice at 11 a.m. on 11 November 1918. In 1919 the peace treaty was signed at Versailles. To the consternation of Germany, she was not invited to take part in the negotiations. This was the first of several bitter blows the German people were forced to endure. When the negotiations between the three allies were complete, Germany's new Weimar Republic was simply told to sign the treaty. As a further insult, Germany would not be allowed to join the new League of Nations until she proved to the three major allies that she would follow the terms of the peace treaty. For the German people, peace was beginning to leave a bitter taste, they felt that the treaty was punitive and unfair, which, unquestionably, it was.

One of the conditions in the treaty was that on the day it was signed the German High Seas Fleet, second only in size to Britain was to become the property of Great Britain. However, its German commanders were so incensed by the terms that they scuttled the entire fleet, which was anchored at the Orkney Islands.

Germany was to lose 13.5 per cent of her land, including her colonies and, with a redistribution of territories, 12.5 per cent of her population. Many of her pre-war colonies had contributed importantly to her economy and the further loss of more than a tenth of her population hit Germany hard in the years to come.

Article 231, known as the 'War Guilt Clause', was bitterly resented among the German population, who saw it as an unfair attempt to place the total blame for the war on Germany and her allies.

Another clause, Article 232, was designed to keep Germany financially weak, the poor relation of Europe, and demanded that she pay France and Britain £6.6 billion in reparation. The Germans pointed out that this clause made it impossible for them to recover economically as it effectively destroyed their potential to build themselves back into an industrial power. Germany was on her knees and it was patently clear that Britain and France intended keeping her there so that she could never again threaten Europe. In an atlas of the Great War, printed after the war, this anonymous quote appears: *'The Allies, by brushing aside their defeated enemy's dismay at the terms imposed, were in fact losing the peace at the moment they won the war.'*

There was no doubt that Lloyd George's demands for compensation and his desire to expand the British Empire by adding the German territories in Africa to his own and Clemenceau's need for revenge and demands for reparation sowed the seeds of resentment and hatred that eventually grew and ripened into the bitter harvest that became the National Socialist Party, led by Adolf Hitler.

General Haig, a man not known for his diplomatic skills, proved on this occasion to see things far more clearly than the two other greedy and vengeful statesmen. In a letter to his wife two weeks before the German army accepted defeat, and during the time when he was urging his commanders to throw everything at the enemy so as to make them *'beg for mercy'*, Haig wrote: *'Our Statesmen should not attempt to humiliate Germany as to produce a desire for revenge in years to come.'*

It was not to be. In little less than a generation, fresh graves were to be dug to accommodate the sons of both sides, so that in death they might lie beside the fathers they never knew in life. We had won the war and lost the peace.

———◈———

A nd so the time had come to say goodbye to England and English friends . . . I kept up a desultory correspondence with the Palmers, Tweedales and Fairmans for some years but it gradually diminished to a letter a year, and then nothing. In 1939 their hospitality was experienced by my sister Marjorie on her ill-fated visit to the UK.

On 29 October 1918 I left England on the S.S. *Borda*, which was carrying mainly walking wounded, some on home leave. She was a very slow and unsteady ship and, as the crew put it, 'would roll in any dry dock'. I was never on her in dry dock but she certainly rolled in glassy or heavy seas, and we had plenty of the latter. We were a few days from Cape Town when, at 11 a.m. on 11 November 1918 the armistice was signed. While elated at the surrender of Germany, we felt cheated of all those joys the world had longed for over four years and for which tens of millions of servicemen and women of many countries had fought and died. We, of course, did our best to stage our own festivities but they were sad rather than joyful. No girls, no beer, no party food, no lights – there was fear that there might be German submarines or other raiders, the crews of which may not have heard the news of the armistice.

A few days later, we rolled into Cape Town harbour where we dropped anchor about a mile from the refuelling wharves. Here we stayed for twelve to fourteen days, waiting our turn to commence coaling by a handful of blacks each filling a basket with coal at a depot about one hundred yards away, then carrying it on their heads over the gangway, then dumping it into the hold and returning to repeat the job over and over for several hours.

The reason for this shortage of labour was the 'Spanish Flu', which was sweeping the world, killing millions in its progress. It was a respiratory disease, and was particularly rife in Africa where the blacks showed little resistance to its ravages, due no doubt to unsanitary living conditions and undernourishment. Lack of hospitals and medical expertise also undoubtedly helped, but there was no known cure for it, and the main efforts were diverted toward preventing it further spreading.

They were dying at the rate of 4000 per day in Cape Town – mostly blacks – and were being buried in quick time in mass graves; or so rumour had it.

Every precaution was taken to stop it spreading to our ship. The wharf was patrolled by civilian and army police and no one other than officials and the black loaders were allowed on or off the ship. Nothing but coal was to be bought, no newspapers, no fruit, which we longed for, particularly oranges. We were, in fact, completely isolated.

Three of our not-so-bright boys decided to break ship for a day in Cape Town. We never saw them again but were later told they had reached the end of the wharf, where they had been collected by the police and marched off to a concentration camp outside the city. Whether they survived, or how long they remained in the camp, I never heard.

In due course, we sailed for home. It was a full two days out from Fremantle that we first smelt Australia when, going on deck after an early breakfast, on a lovely breeze from the east we picked up a faint smell of eucalyptus. There was an unashamed tear in most eyes and many men developed hacking coughs.

We were warned by numbers of the crew that the Bight could be difficult because of the heavy ground swells sometimes encountered there, and they considered that, in a notorious roller like the *Borda*, it could be dangerous. Cheerful counsel when we were so near to home.

Their advice proved to be well founded as about halfway across we were hit without warning by a monster. We were lunching at the time the ship began to list. The list continued, quite slowly, and all believed she would roll over. I had no idea for how long the roll continued, it seemed for minutes, but was perhaps twenty to thirty seconds, until, eventually, she trembled and slowly began to right herself. There was no panic but several arms and collarbones and a leg or two were broken in the roll. The captain was reported to have said that he thought she would not right herself.

Nothing else of any importance took place and we arrived at Adelaide on 16 December 1918. South Australians and Victorians disembarked on the seventeenth and the Victorians later took a train to Melbourne arriving there at about ten or eleven a.m., where my mother and sister Marjorie and an assortment of female relatives were waiting for me. All Victorians were given fifteen-day leave passes.

Word of our coming must have been signalled along the route to Melbourne and at every stop of ten minutes or more the local ladies provided a regular banquet of ham, chicken and cakes laden with thick cream, that was spread out on trestle tables on the platform. Unfortunately, it poured with rain for most of the journey and, as few of the stations had much cover, the poor ladies became soaked.

The most lavish meal of the lot, however, was at home in Ballarat which my sister, Birdie, had stayed home preparing. It included a large crayfish, and that proved my undoing. I was violently ill during the night. It was many years before I could again look at a cray without feeling ill.

It was great to be home again, with all its love and comforts, but the four years in the army had left its mark and I was soon uneasy and unsettled. I was back early and not many of the fellows I had known who had survived the war had as yet returned.

Australia was not the land of Heavenly Happiness we had built up in our minds. There was great bitterness between the families of those whose sons or daughters and, in many cases, fathers had served in the forces – particularly those who had members killed or wounded – and those who had stayed at home. That, I suppose, was inevitable, considering the white feathers that had been distributed to men in civilian clothes by overenthusiastic females, sometimes to men who had been rejected because of some physical disability often undistinguishable and by the bitterness of the campaign for conscription. It took many years for those old sores to heal, and the healing process was not helped by the policy of 'Preference for Returned Men' in employment which was passed through Federal Parliament and became law.

The Sisterian issue was also rampant. It had become not so much Protestant versus Catholic as a national problem of Irish versus English. The man who was mainly responsible for the hatred between the faiths was Archbishop Mannix, the primate of the Catholic Church in Victoria. He brought his anti-British hatred with him from Ireland, where he was a strong supporter of the republican Sinn Fein Society. I do not know whether or not he was a good churchman, but I do know he carried his hatred too far as the following anecdote shows: he announced in the press (the year would have been in the very early 1920s) that in the forthcoming St Patrick's Day march through the streets of Melbourne the

Union Jack – which was normally flown, with other sym-
bolic flags at the head of the march – would not appear.
Patriotic fever was still high and he was promptly told by
the authorities (maybe the police) that the Union Jack must
lead the march. The flag was carried by a staggering down-
and-out methylated-spirit drinker, with five VC winners
forming the front rank of the march.

One of Mannix's greatest supporters was the gambling
millionaire, John Wren, whose home adjoined the archbishop's palace. He (the archbishop) lived – and retained –
his archbishopric until he was almost a hundred, and it was
not until his death that the hatred started to disappear . . .

On about the second of January 1919 I reported to
Caulfield Military Hospital, only to discover it was overcrowded and that it was decided that all walking cases
would go to Mont Park Military Hospital at Macleod, a mile
or two beyond Heidelberg. The hospital proved to be rather
desolate, consisting of ten or a dozen two-storeyed wards,
built in a low-growing scrub area, and was originally
intended as a civilian mental hospital; in fact, one or two of
the wards were already occupied as such.

I spent four and a half months there before being discharged on 19 May 1919 as being 'medically unfit, not due
to misconduct'. A peculiar wording to describe a discharge
due to wounds, but such was the way of the army in 1919.
My total service was 1446 days, of which 1252 were in service abroad.

What Roy described was very common. Towards the end of Gallipoli a general despondency had taken over the men in the trenches, they'd tried and it had not been for a lack of courage that they'd failed. The slaughter at The Nek seemed to be the last straw and after this they finally lost any remaining faith they may have retained for the leadership. To put it bluntly, they were too sick, too weary and too discouraged to continue fighting. Statistically speaking the health of the Anzacs had collapsed.

In September 1915 a survey judged three-quarters of the men in the trenches totally unfit for active service. In those times, when stoicism was expected of men, such a high percentage of unfit indicates that, if judged by today's standards, they should all have long since been removed from active duty.

Today we would see much of this as post-traumatic stress disorder but at that time there was no such term and it was simply put down to nerves. Or as one soldier at Gallipoli put it: *'Our nerves are getting very nervy . . .'*

Later, when men returned from Europe and many began to behave in an anti-social manner or became depressed, the condition became known as 'shell shock' for which there appeared to be no treatment other than the proverbial shed in the backyard. Returned veterans, when their 'nerves' got too bad, would retire to the shed in the backyard, often for days at a time. Mum would tell the kids, 'Dad's in the shed, it's his nerves, best to leave him alone until he comes out of it.' Other veterans would drink excessively during these times with concomitant disastrous effects on family life. It was not until the end of World War II that we began to realise that the act of war has an ongoing effect on society and can have disastrous effects on family life and the attitudes of the generation following. After Vietnam we finally nailed this psychological effect as PTSD and began to treat it, although the Australian government, not wanting to accept responsibility, held out until the 1980s before they finally acknowledged the on-going effects caused by post-traumatic stress disorder.

———◆———

After two to three weeks, I rejoined the bank at Ballarat but, at the end of the third month, was transferred to Kingston, a rather derelict settlement of some twenty-three cottages, in addition to two hotels, a school, a post office and a church and the offices of the Shire of Creswick, which, a few years later, were transferred to Creswick, their rightful place.

I resented the move, which was due to the National Training Service requiring the attendance of my predecessor at Creswick for training on the days on which the Newlyn agency of Kingston Branch three miles away had to be opened. As the branch staff consisted of a manager and a general dogsbody – me – it was unremarkable.

There was nothing to do after work but to drink with the locals until well into the night, and that formed my usual routine until I had the great good fortune to meet Jessie Dorothea Johannsen from Allendale, a skeletal mining settlement a little over a mile from Kingston. I immediately fell in love and spent at least three nights of the week visiting her on foot. Her family moved to Melbourne early in 1920 and we were married in the Scots Church, Collins Street, Melbourne, on 16 March 1920.

I was drawing a salary of £230 a year, shortly to be increased to £250 on my transfer to Castlemaine.

We had difficult times but saw them through. (And, after seventy years at the time of writing – February 1990 – we are just as much, or more, in love than we were in 1920.)

Whilst at Castlemaine, our two children were born Leonard Rupert (Jock) in 1921 and Sheila Rose (Sheish) in 1924.

We took an active part in local affairs at Castlemaine. I was active in the Returned Soldiers League (then the Returned Soldiers' Imperial League of Australia) and was its president in 1925 as well as secretary of the local tennis club, a member of the football team and, amongst other interests, a member of a unique organisation, the Odd Volo Club, in other words, a literary society.

Late in 1925, I was transferred to Bendigo and the rest was a run-of-the-mill career. To Melbourne in 1928 to work in several branches there until in 1936 I was appointed to manage the Footscray branch. Five years there and then in 1941 Goulburn, NSW. Five years there and then to St Kilda in 1946, then to Newcastle, NSW, in 1948, and after the merger of The Bank of Australasia and The Union Bank of Australia in 1951, to Adelaide to the management of what, to that date, had been the main city branch . . . of the former. In 1957, at the age of sixty, I retired.

Of all the places we lived in, Goulburn and Adelaide remain my favourites. Although one was a small country city in a predominantly wool-growing area, and the other a state capital, they had much in common; both ultra-conservative by Australian standards but, when you got to know them and their people, both warm-hearted and friendly . . .

Such a lot happened to our family during those five years in Goulburn. For the first four years, the Second World War was raging and our two lovely children joined the services – Jock in the navy as a radar operator and Sheila in the W.A.A.A.F. (Women's Australian Auxiliary Air Force) as a wireless operator stationed at Wagga Wagga, NSW. She joined at eighteen but I refused permission for her to go abroad, although that was unnecessary as girls of that age were not sent overseas and their skills were also needed in Australia. Fortunately, they both came through unscathed . . .

The family tragedy of the period was the death at sea by enemy submarine action of my much loved sister, Marjorie, returning to Australia from England in 1943.

Another event of great note during our years in Goulburn

was the advent of Sub-Lieutenant (later Lieutenant Commander) Hadyn Pryce Smith of the Royal Navy. He was a fighter pilot on H.M.S. *Indomitable* (an aircraft carrier) and came to Goulburn to play a social game of cricket against a local team while his ship was in Sydney. He was introduced to Sheila, who was on weekend leave from Wagga, by his hostess for the weekend, Mrs Vera Ford of Goulburn, and they fell in love; just as simple as that.

Hadyn returned to England after the surrender of the Japanese but returned to Australia as soon as possible and obtained his discharge from the Navy here in 1946, and they were married at Heidelberg later that year, soon after which I was transferred to St Kilda.

Hadyn obtained a position with an insurance company and Sheila worked in a local pharmacy. A year later, Hadyn was admitted to the Medical School at the University of Melbourne, and began long years of study which he completed successfully. Eventually they settled in Geelong. They gave us two lovely grandchildren – both girls, Miranda and Liza, who in turn have given us six equally lovely great-grandchildren. Mandy married Colin Bridges and Liza married John Mill.

After much heart-searching Jessie and I decided to move to Geelong. Jock, who married a lovely Sydney girl, Betty Moore, in 1948 had returned to G. J. Coles and was on the move every second year, so we took a sad farewell to Adelaide and friends and settled in Geelong.

Jock made steady progress with Coles and, after running a number of branches, was appointed to the management of their Adelaide city branch, shortly after we left. He was there for some years when, at his request, he returned to Victoria and the management of the Prahran branch. We grew to love Betty very dearly, but sadly she died in 1986. They had three equally lovely children, two girls and a boy – Jacqueline and twins, Robert and Georgina. Betty's death left us all devastated. She was a wonderful wife, mother and daughter-in-law, and was greatly loved by her in-laws.

Jock was fortunate enough to meet and marry another fine woman, Mai Plummer, a few years later . . .

We have lived an uneventful life in Geelong, having arrived too late in life to make friends easily or to take an active part in local affairs but have had the great joy of watching our grandchildren grow up, and the experience is being repeated with our great-grandchildren.

My final chapter will be written in a few weeks' time after my return from Gallipoli, to which I am going, at the age of ninety-two, as a guest of the Commonwealth with fifty-eight other Gallipoli veterans for the seventy-fifth anniversary of the landing of the Australians and New Zealanders at Anzac Cove on 25 April 1915.

In 1990, Roy Kyle, when an old man, returned to Gallipoli with other survivors. While there, a Turk approached him and asked, 'Why did you try to invade our country?'

Roy paused for a few moments, perhaps not having an

Roy Kyle

immediate answer. 'We were part of the British Empire,' he suggested at last.

The Turk smiled, then added, 'We had an empire once.'

Roy would later say that he saw the essential truth in it. The sun does finally set on every empire. Everything comes to an end, nothing lasts forever. War never has nor ever will solve the problems of the human race.

FAMILY ACKNOWLEDGEMENTS

Roy's family wish to express their love and gratitude to Roy for the legacy of this book. At the age of eighty-nine he began to record his recollections and reminiscences of events in his life for the benefit of his family and friends. It is ironic and sad that none of his immediate family (neither his wife Jessie [nee Johannsen], his son Jock, nor his daughter Sheila Smith) is alive to see his book. However his spirit lives on in his five grandchildren and thirteen great-grandchildren and in his country.

Over several years Roy sat for many hours at his desk and recorded with fountain pen, in five school exercise books, his recollections of his early years. On the inside cover of one of the exercise books he had written:

> *Memories come surging back*
> *Along the road from yesteryear*

Thanks to the following people:

Lambis Englezos who shared with Roy, in Roy's later years, an interest in military matters. Lambis's enthusiasm and determination ensured that Roy's work started on its path to publication. His interest and help continued throughout its journey. Without his efforts the book may never have seen the light of day; Bryce Courtenay who saw merit in Roy's story and encouraged the project from its early stages. His editing, researches and annotations have added so much to the work; Mandy Bridges and Liza Mill, my daughters, for their love of Roy and his dearest wife Jessie and for their wisdom, advice and patience during the book's evolution; Colin Bridges, my son-in-law, who arranged legal matters for the family; Lesley Bright who typed the first draft of the book from Roy's longhand – a task which required great patience; Roberta Ashby of Radio 3RPH who carried out some editing of the early draft; Sylvain Macrez of Saint-Pol-sur-Ternoise, France, who assisted with researching of the correct spelling of place and battlefield names in Belgium and France; Mary Boardman of Canberra who supplied information and photographs; Marlene Allen at Allen and Kemsley Publishing for her kind assistance; Steven Siewert for his wonderful photograph of Roy aged ninety-seven; The Australian War Memorial staff, and especially Joanne Smedley for her help with identifying a special photograph of Roy and his trench mortar crew; Dr Peter Jackman for his help in keeping Roy in good writing form over very many years. Finally our special thanks to Robert Sessions, Kay Ronai, Saskia Adams and Marina Messiha from Penguin Books for their very generous and friendly assistance, which we have greatly appreciated.

At the age of ninety-two Roy returned to Gallipoli in 1990 to attend the commemoration of the 75th anniversary of the campaign. With his advancing years he did not resume his writing.

Every effort has been made to ensure the accuracy of details in Roy's writing.

Dr Hadyn Smith, on behalf of Roy's family

BRYCE COURTENAY'S ACKNOWLEDGEMENTS

I wish to thank all those people who are mentioned in the bibliography of this book and without whom it would have been quite impossible to write. Obviously a book of this nature contains several hundred quotes and there may be a few which have not been attributed. If, as a reader or a writer, you come across an unattributed quote, would you kindly let my publishers know so that the author may be given the credit due to him or her.

My thanks to researchers, Joyce Bradley, Clare Coney and Margaret Barca, and Bill Fogarty for reading the manuscript.

BIBLIOGRAPHY

Adam-Smith, P. *The Anzacs* (Penguin Books, Ringwood, 1991)

Austin, R. *As Rough as Bags: A History of the 6th Battalion, 1st AIF)* (R. J. & S. B. Austin, Australia, 1992)

Australian Bureau of Statistics, *Commonwealth Year Book, 1901–09* (Australian Bureau of Statistics, Melbourne, 1911)

Barnett, C. *The Great War* (Penguin Books, Harmondsworth, 2000 edition)

Bean, C. E. W. *ANZAC to Amiens* (Australian War Memorial, 1983 edition)

Bell, A. D. (ed) *An Anzac's War Diary: The Story of Sergeant Richardson* (Rigby, Melbourne, 1981)

Beaumont, J. (ed) *Australia's War, 1914–18* (Allen & Unwin, Sydney, 1995)

Carlyon, L. *Gallipoli* (Macmillian, Sydney, 2001)

Clare, J. D. *I Was There: First World War* (Random House, London, 1994)

Cliff, P. (ed) *The Endless Playground* (National Library of Australia, Canberra, 2000)

Coulthard-Clark, C. *Where Australians Fought* (Allen & Unwin, Sydney, 1998)

Cuffley, P. A. *Chandeliers & Billy Tea 1880–1940* (The Five Mile Press, Victoria, 1984)

Dennis, P., et al. *The Oxford Companion to Australian Military History* (Oxford University Press, Melbourne, 1995)

Downing, W. H. *To the Last Ridge* (Duffy & Snellgrove, Sydney, 1998)

Gammage, B. *The Broken Years* (Penguin Books, Melbourne, 1974)

Grey, J. *A Military History of Australia* (Cambridge University Press, Melbourne, 1990)

Grey, J. *Volume 1: The Australian Army* (Oxford University Press, Melbourne, 2001)

Harvey, W. J. *The Red and White Diamond* (Alexander McCubbin, Melbourne, 1921)

Hogg, I. V. *Mortars* (The Crowood Press, London, 2001)

Horne, D. *The Story of the Australian People* (Reader's Digest, Sydney, 1972)

Johnston, S. *Experiences of the Great War, 1914–1918* (Longman Cheshire, Melbourne, 1987)

Kerr, G. *Private War: Personal Records of the Anzacs in the Great War* (Oxford University Press, Melbourne, 2000)

Larkins, J., Howard B. *The Young Australians: Australian Children Since 1788* (Rigby, Australia, 1981)

Livesey, A. *The Viking Atlas of World War I* (Viking, Penguin Books, London, 1994)

Macdonald, L. *They Called it Passchendaele* (Macmillan, London, 1983 edition)

MacDougall, A. K. *ANZACS: Australians at War* (Reed Books, Sydney, 1991)

McKernan, M. *Padre, Australian Chaplains in Gallipoli and France* (Allen & Unwin, Sydney 1986)

McKernan, M., & Browne, M. *Australia. Two Cultures of War and Peace* (Australian War Memorial in association with Allen & Unwin, Sydney, 1988).

McLachlan, R., Bundock, A., & Wood, M. *Discovering Gallipoli, Research Guide* (Times Past Productions, Bathurst, NSW, for the Australian War Memorial, 1990)

McQueen, H. *Social Sketches of Australia* (Penguin, Ringwood, 1991 ed.)

Niall, B., Britain, I. (eds) *The Oxford Book of Australian Schooldays* (Oxford University Press, Melbourne, 1997)

Reader's Digest Services, *Australia's Yesterdays: A Look at our Recent Past* (Reader's Digest, Sydney, 1974)

Robson, L. L. *Australia & the Great War* (Macmillan, Melbourne, 1970)

Stephens, T. *The Last Anzacs: Gallipoli 1915* (Allen & Kemsley Publishing, NSW, 1996)

Unit War Diaries. 1914–18 War. 24th Infantry Battalion

Welborn, S.   *Lords of Death* (Fremantle Arts Centre Press, 1982)

Winter, J.M.   *The Experience of World War I* (Macmillan, London, 1988)

MAGAZINES
Reveille

INTERNET
Treaty of Versailles
www.foundingdocs.gov.au

ABC Television Documentaries: The Battleships
www.abc.net.au/documentaries/program

Conscription
www.awm.gov.au

PHOTOGRAPH ACKNOWLEDGEMENTS

Photographs from page 2 to page 7 reproduced by kind permission of the Australian War Memorial.

Photograph of Roy at age 97 taken by Steven Siewert and reproduced by kind permission of the Fairfax Photo Library.